DC COMICS
THE ULTIMATE
CHARACTER GUIDE

Written by
Brandon T. Snider

INTRODUCTION

In the DC Universe, super heroes, villains, aliens, and cyborgs clash, team up, plot, and sleuth. This book will tell you all about them. Batman, Wonder Woman, Superman, and your other favorite super heroes are all here, as well as lesser known alumni such as Blue Beetle, Plastic Man, and Sandman. You'll meet all kinds of villains, from the cold-hearted Lex Luthor to the deadly Cyborg Superman. You'll discover teams whose mission is to save the world and others intent on destroying it. The DC Universe is a big place. Enjoy exploring!

CONTENTS

This book contains more than 200 heroes and villains from the DC Universe and every page is filled with amazing facts and stats. The characters and teams are arranged in alphabetical order according to their first name or title. For example, Harley Quinn, the Joker's girlfriend, is under "H," Professor Hugo Strange is under "P," and Mad Hatter is under "M." Use the contents list below to zoom straight to each character or team, and start learning fascinating facts about the weird and wonderful people who populate the DC Universe!

ADAM STRANGE
GALACTIC CHAMPION

Adam Strange's life changed forever the day the mysterious Zeta Beam transported him from his home on Earth to the faraway planet of Rann. Now settled on Rann with a wife and child, Adam protects the planet while also fighting villains all over the cosmos. He often works with the Justice League of America.

VITAL STATS

REAL NAME Adam Strange

OCCUPATION Adventurer, Hero

HEIGHT 6ft

WEIGHT 175 lbs

BASE Rann, Ranagar

ALLIES Justice League of America

FOES Starbreaker, Lady Styx

Adam uses a Rannian ray gun to defend himself in battle.

His rocket pack propels him through the cosmos.

The Zeta Beam can teleport Adam anywhere in the universe.

FAMILY MAN

Adam Strange spends most of his time defending the galaxy, but he prefers the quiet life on Rann with his loving wife, Alanna, and their daughter Aleea. Adam often disagrees with his wife's father, Sardath, who created the Zeta Beam technology that first brought him to Rann.

POWERS: On Earth, Adam was a brilliant archaeologist who studied the relics of the past. His interplanetary adventures have since made him an expert on aliens and other worlds. Adam wears a suit and helmet that protect him from the harsh conditions in space. He's also a skilled fighter.

ALFRED PENNYWORTH

BUTLER TO BATMAN

Alfred spent time in the British Secret Service.

Alfred Pennyworth has been the Wayne family's trusted butler for many years. When young Bruce Wayne lost his parents, Alfred helped the boy through his most difficult times. Later, Bruce became Batman, and Alfred remained not only his butler but also his advisor, mentor, and friend.

He takes pride in being perfectly dressed at all times.

VITAL STATS

REAL NAME Alfred Pennyworth
OCCUPATION Butler
HEIGHT 6ft
WEIGHT 160 lbs
BASE Wayne Manor, Gotham City
ALLIES Batman, Robin
FOES The Joker, The Penguin

His everyday duties include maintaining Batman's costumes and equipment.

POWERS: Alfred has assisted Batman on many cases, using his acting ability as well as various disguises to impersonate people. He is skilled in many different fighting techniques, and has a vast knowledge of medicine which he uses to treat Batman's injuries. Alfred is also a superb chef and, of course, the perfect butler!

KEEPER OF THE CAVE

Trusty Alfred maintains Wayne Manor as well as the Batcave—Batman's high-tech hideout below the residence. During a recent absence by the Dark Knight, Alfred even led the heroic team called the Outsiders, sending them on covert missions across the globe.

AMANDA WALLER
THE WALL

Amanda Waller is the tough-talking leader of the secretive Task Force X, a team of former villains whom she sends on spy missions. Waller has a deep distrust of the world's super heroes and has made it known that she will not hesitate to take them down—using any means at her disposal.

VITAL STATS
REAL NAME Amanda Waller
OCCUPATION Director of Task Force X
HEIGHT 5ft 9in
WEIGHT 225 lbs
BASE Belle Reve Prison, Louisiana
ALLIES Suicide Squad, Checkmate
FOES Justice League of America

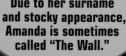

Her sharp mind and steely determination make her a natural leader.

Due to her surname and stocky appearance, Amanda is sometimes called "The Wall."

CHEMICAL WARFARE
While on a mission to take down an evil organization, Amanda Waller discovered a way to mentally operate the toxic robot Chemo, using a remote control helmet. Waller enjoyed controlling the chemical monster, and even shaped his malleable form to resemble her likeness.

POWERS: Because of her various affiliations, Amanda Waller has a vast network of secret information at her disposal and does not hesitate to use the knowledge she gathers to destroy her enemies. Despite her weight and bulk, Amanda is also an excellent hand-to-hand fighter.

AMAZO
ABOMINABLE ANDROID

Amazo sometimes takes on the physical features of the heroes whose powers he absorbs.

Amazo is an evil android created by the mad scientist Professor Ivo to aid in his quest for immortality. Amazo was originally programmed to absorb the abilities of the Justice League of America, whose energies Ivo hoped would bring him eternal life. However, Amazo can absorb the energies of *any* super-being.

VITAL STATS

REAL NAME Amazo
OCCUPATION Android, Villain
HEIGHT 5ft 11in
WEIGHT 485 lbs
BASE Mobile
ALLIES Professor Ivo
FOES Justice League of America, Hourman

Amazo's body is constantly upgrading to become more powerful.

ANDROID ATTACK
When the Red Tornado's spirit was separated from his android form, Amazo gained control of the hero's body and took it on a wild rampage. It was left to the JLA to shut him down and salvage their friend's body.

POWERS: Amazo can absorb and use the powers of any hero, including Superman's strength, Batman's brilliant mind, and Green Lantern's ability to create energy constructs. Although he has evolved over through the years, Amazo still absorbs the weaknesses—as well as the powers—of the heroes he encounters.

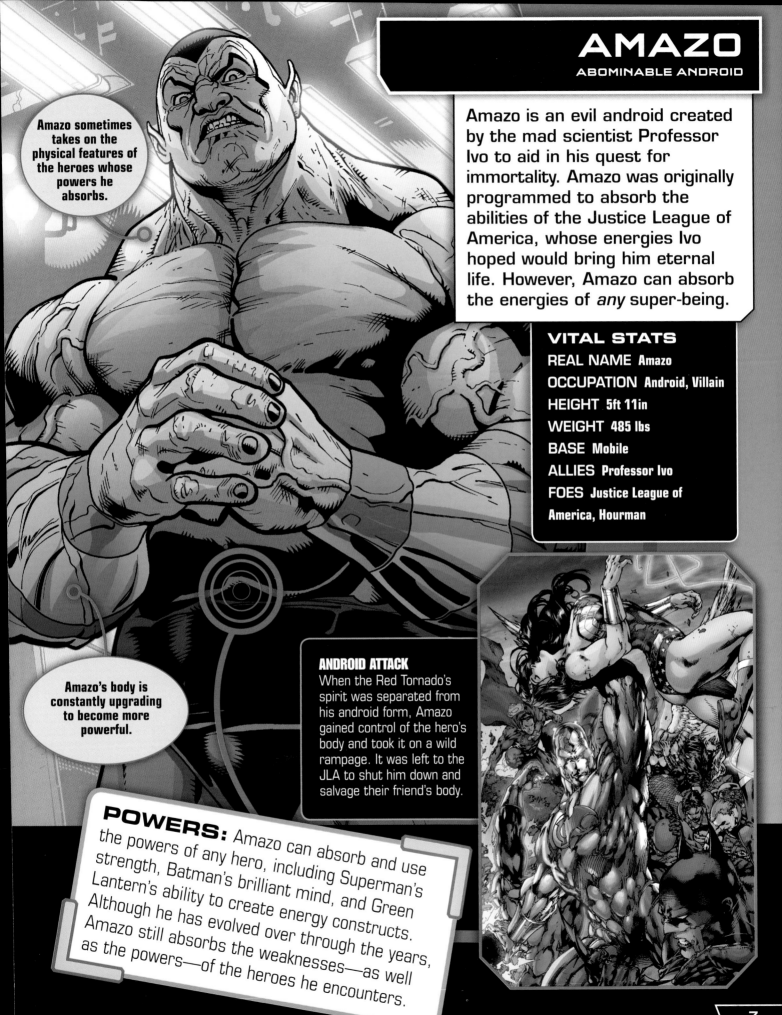

ANIMAL MAN

ONE MAN ZOO

Buddy Baker was a stuntman in the movies until the day he was given experimental powers by a group of aliens. They turned him into Animal Man—a hero who can replicate the powers and abilities of any animal on Earth. Buddy may be a bit of an animal now, but he's still just a family man at heart!

VITAL STATS

REAL NAME Buddy Baker
OCCUPATION Father, Hero
HEIGHT 5ft 11in
WEIGHT 175 lbs
BASE San Diego
ALLIES Justice League of America, Starfire
FOES Lady Styx, Mirror Master

Animal Man wears a leather jacket because he thinks it's cool.

Animal Man can also absorb the powers of alien creatures while in space.

LOST IN SPACE

Animal Man, Starfire, and Adam Strange once became lost in space while tracking down a deadly alien slave taker named Lady Styx. The trio became very close friends and, after they returned to Earth, Starfire even lived with Animal Man and his family for a time.

POWERS: Animal Man taps into the Lifeweb, an energy that connects all living things on the planet Earth. This allows him to sense the animals around him and take on their special abilities. He can soar as high as an eagle, run as fast as a cheetah, and has the proportionate strength of a spider. He's also a strong fighter.

ANTI-MONITOR
WRATHFUL WATCHER

In the event known as the Crisis on Infinite Earths, the power-hungry being called the Anti-Monitor merged multiple worlds, warping both time and space for his devious purposes. Now he quietly watches from his lair in a parallel universe, waiting for the perfect time to bring chaos to the universe once again.

The Anti-Monitor has only rarely been heard to speak.

If the Anti-Monitor's armor is damaged, his life force may leak out.

VITAL STATS

REAL NAME None
OCCUPATION Conqueror, Villain
HEIGHT Indeterminable
WEIGHT Indeterminable
BASE Qward
ALLIES Sinestro Corps
FOES Heroes

CORPS POWER
The Anti-Monitor's body was once destroyed, but robots known as the Manhunters rebuilt him and he became a part of the evil Sinestro Corps. In this role, he gained control of the Green Lantern energy source. The Green Lantern Corps had a tough battle to get it back!

POWERS: The Anti-Monitor is a giant, able to expand in height until he is hundreds of feet tall. In addition, he has super-strength and endurance. Using his armor, the Anti-Monitor can fire electric bolts and absorb the energies of the heroes he seeks to destroy—an ability that makes him virtually indestructible!

AQUALAD
AMPHIBIOUS ACE

Aqualad is the lost son of the villain Black Manta and has only recently found out about his amazing powers. Black Manta has since tried to reclaim his son, but thankfully, Aquaman has taken the young hero under his wing to protect him and ensure Aqualad never falls prey to his father's evil ways.

VITAL STATS
REAL NAME Jackson Hyde
OCCUPATION Hero
HEIGHT 5ft 9in
WEIGHT 170 lbs
BASE New Mexico
ALLIES Aquaman, Mera
FOES Black Manta

He carries waterbearers that help him to focus his power.

Aqualad has webbed hands which aid him in underwater travel.

WATER WIELDER
An ancient Atlantean prophecy foretold the heroic path laid out for Aqualad. As the first outsider to be born in Xebel, a realm where exiles from Atlantis dwelt, he was destined to unlock a chest. The devices inside would allow him to access his wonderful powers.

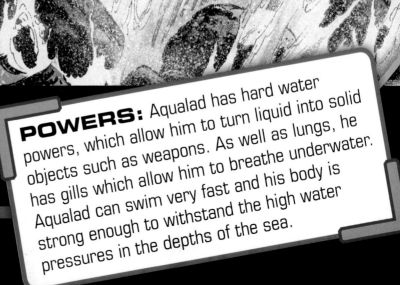

POWERS: Aqualad has hard water powers, which allow him to turn liquid into solid objects such as weapons. As well as lungs, he has gills which allow him to breathe underwater. Aqualad can swim very fast and his body is strong enough to withstand the high water pressures in the depths of the sea.

KAANNG

AQUAMAN
KING OF THE SEAS

He is the only person in Atlantis to have blond hair.

Aquaman was abandoned by his parents and raised by a lighthouse keeper, not knowing where he really came from. After discovering that he was from the underwater city of Atlantis, Aquaman returned to his home as a hero. Recognized to be of royal blood, he now defends the city as its proud king.

Aquaman's left hand was once replaced with a harpoon.

VITAL STATS
REAL NAME Arthur Curry, Orin
OCCUPATION King, Hero
HEIGHT 6ft 1in
WEIGHT 225 lbs
BASE Atlantis
ALLIES Mera, Aqualad
FOES Black Manta, Ocean Master

POWER COUPLE
Aquaman's wife, Queen Mera, is from Xebel, the world of exiled Atlanteans. She was originally sent by her father, the ruler of Xebel, to kill the King of the Seas. Instead, Mera fell deeply in love with Aquaman and remained in Atlantis as his wife.

POWERS: Aquaman uses his gills to breathe underwater, and can also communicate telepathically with all forms of sea life. He has incredible strength and can swim at very high speeds. Thanks to his colleagues in the Justice League, Aquaman has also learned many different fighting skills.

ARES
GOD OF WAR

Ares is the mythical Greek God of War. Cold, cruel, and deadly, he relishes bloodshed and enjoys causing trouble outside the realm of the gods. Ares is always trying to bring about the destruction of the human world and especially loves to torment his arch enemy, the peace-loving Wonder Woman.

His helmet is like that of an ancient Greek warrior, but with added spikes.

Ares wears a heavy blue suit of armor that is almost indestructible.

VITAL STATS

REAL NAME Ares

OCCUPATION God of War

HEIGHT 6ft 10in

WEIGHT 460 lbs

BASE Olympus

ALLIES Phobos, Eris, Deimos

FOES Wonder Woman

DUKE OF DECEPTION
Ares will often change his form into that of a regular human man in order to gain the trust of his enemies. Though many are coaxed into thinking Ares's intentions are good, Wonder Woman knows the God of War can't be trusted.

POWERS: Ares is a fierce fighter who is protected in battle by his mystical armor. Because he is the God of War, his very presence brings out the anger in those he comes into contact with, causing them to battle one another. Ares—a master manipulator—does not fail to use this to his advantage.

ARSENAL
WEAPONS MASTER

He carries an array of deadly knives with him for protection.

When young Roy Harper lost his father, he was taken in by a Navajo chief named Brave Bow who taught him archery. Roy's skills won him a place as Green Arrow's sidekick, Speedy, and he later joined the Teen Titans. Now known as Arsenal, Roy remains a quick-thinking hotshot who often gets into trouble.

VITAL STATS
REAL NAME Roy Harper
OCCUPATION Hero
HEIGHT 5ft 11in
WEIGHT 195 lbs
BASE New York City
ALLIES Teen Titans, Justice League of America
FOES Cheshire, Fearsome Five

He has worn a bionic arm since his real arm was cut off by an enemy.

RISE OF RED ARROW
In one of the Justice League of America's lineup changes, Arsenal was offered membership instead of his mentor, Green Arrow. Far from being resentful at being left out, Green Arrow gave Arsenal his blessing. Arsenal joined the team, going into battle with them under the new name of Red Arrow.

POWERS: Arsenal learned many of his skills from Green Arrow and is one of the most accurate and deadly archers in the world. He can turn anything into a weapon, which he then uses to protect himself in battle. Arsenal is also a superb athlete, a skilled fighter, and natural born leader.

ARTEMIS
WARRIOR WOMAN

Artemis is an Amazon from the lost tribe of the Bana-Mighdall. She is a fierce competitor and once won a contest to find a replacement for Princess Diana as the Amazons' representative in the outside world. For a brief time, Artemis served as Wonder Woman, but her aggressive attitude soon lost her the role.

VITAL STATS

REAL NAME Artemis
OCCUPATION Queen, Hero
HEIGHT 6ft
WEIGHT 166 lbs
BASE Themyscira
ALLIES Wonder Woman, Hippolyta
FOES Ares, Circe

She has died and been resurrected several times.

Artemis wields a sharp sword, which she does not hesitate to use in battle.

THE CONTEST
The Amazon queen, Hippolyta, had a murky vision of the future in which she saw Wonder Woman perish. Wishing to protect her daughter Diana, who was the current Wonder Woman, Hippolyta held a contest to choose a new Amazon champion. Artemis won the contest and became the new Wonder Woman.

POWERS: Artemis is a superb tactician and has commanded the armies of the Bana-Mighdall in many battles. She has trained in numerous fighting styles and is an expert in hand-to-hand combat. Artemis is adept at wielding a sword, but often prefers to defend a bow and arrow.

THE ATOM

MIGHTY MITE

Brilliant scientist Ray Palmer uses the power of a fallen meteor fragment to shrink down and fight crime as the Atom. While small in size, the Atom is quick on his feet—and super smart too! He applies his knowledge of science to solving mysteries as a member of the Justice League of America.

An atom symbol appears in the center of his mask.

The Atom's costume shrinks and grows with him.

He controls his shrinking abilities via his belt.

VITAL STATS

REAL NAME Ray Palmer
OCCUPATION Scientist, Hero
HEIGHT 6ft
WEIGHT 180 lbs
BASE Ivy Town
ALLIES Justice League of America
FOES Eclipso, Chronos

POWERS:
The Atom's belt contains matter from a White Dwarf Star, which gives him the ability to shrink down to subatomic size while retaining his full strength. He sometimes uses his medical knowledge to shrink down and perform very precise surgical procedures, and often travels around by riding telephone signals.

SWORD OF THE ATOM
During a low point in his personal life, the Atom decided to drop out and travel to the jungles of South America. He couldn't give up being a hero, and soon found himself helping a group of tiny aliens to defeat their enemies.

ATOM-SMASHER
GIANT GUARDIAN

Atom-Smasher is a powerhouse of a hero. At his normal height he towers over others, and when he changes in size he becomes a real giant! His fiery temper has sometimes led him to clash with his friends. However, he's proven himself a true hero time and again, serving proudly in the Justice Society of America.

VITAL STATS

REAL NAME Albert Julian Rothstein

OCCUPATION Hero

HEIGHT 7ft 6in

WEIGHT 297 lbs

BASE New York City

ALLIES Justice Society of America

FOES Black Adam, Injustice Society

Atom-Smasher wears a wrestler's mask to conceal his identity.

NUKLON
Before he became known as Atom-Smasher, Albert had another identity as a hero called Nuklon. Nuklon was a member of Infinity Inc., a team of younger heroes who wanted to carry on the Justice Society's legacy during a time when the Society had disbanded.

POWERS: Atom-Smasher is incredibly strong at his normal size, and even stronger when he grows into his giant form. He's been known to grow to over 50 feet, but his true limits are unknown. Atom-Smasher is also a strong hand-to-hand fighter, having been trained by the Justice Society's Wildcat.

AZRAEL
AVENGING ANGEL

Azrael is the name of the man chosen to protect the ancient religious sect known as the Order of Purity. He has battled the forces of evil for centuries wearing the Suit of Sorrows, a set of mystical chain mail armor. Now operating out of Gotham City, Azrael assists Batman in his war on crime.

The Suit of Sorrows was forged hundreds of years ago.

VITAL STATS
REAL NAME Michael Washington Lane
OCCUPATION Police Officer, Vigilante
HEIGHT 6ft
WEIGHT 175 lbs
BASE Gotham City
ALLIES Batman
FOES Talia al Ghul

Azrael uses the flaming Swords of Sin and Salvation to defend himself.

AGENT OF THE BAT
Before Michael, there was another hero named Azrael. He was Jean Paul Valley, a man who worked with Batman on a case and trained with him for a time. This Azrael even stepped in to protect Gotham City when the Dark Knight was out of action after Bane broke his back.

POWERS: The Suit of Sorrows grants its wearer incredible strength and speed, but it is very dangerous. If the wearer's soul is not pure, the suit will drive him insane. Azrael himself has to fight to keep his sanity. Police training in the Gotham City Police Department, has made Azrael a skilled hand-to-hand fighter.

BANE
BAT-BREAKER

Bane grew up on the island prison of Santa Prisca, suffering for the crimes of his father. The child knew only the pain of violence—but as his anger at the outside world grew, so did his strength. Finally becoming a free man, the now-deadly Bane came to Gotham City where he faced off against Batman.

Bane wears a mask to frighten his opponents—not to conceal his identity.

Bane was once addicted to Venom but he no longer is.

VITAL STATS
REAL NAME Unknown
OCCUPATION Villain
HEIGHT 6ft 8in
WEIGHT 350 lbs
BASE Gotham City, Mobile
ALLIES Secret Six, Ra's al Ghul
FOES Batman

BREAKING THE BAT
Bane once destroyed the walls of Arkham Asylum, Gotham City's prison for the criminally insane. Hordes of villains were unleashed from its cells. As Batman desperately tried to corral them, Bane attacked—and broke the Dark Knight's back!

POWERS: Venom, a dangerous chemical, gives Bane incredible strength and allows him to heal quickly. Bane is a brilliant tactician and has mastered many different fighting styles. It's been noted that Bane is also highly intelligent, having studied many subjects, ⸺ience during his time in prison.

BATGIRL
DARING DEFENDER

Although Stephanie Brown is the daughter of the villainous Cluemaster, she has not followed in his criminal footsteps. In fact, she has dedicated her life to stopping crime in all its forms as Batgirl. Trained by the Dark Knight himself, Batgirl uses an array of weapons to help protect Gotham City.

Like other members of the Batman family, she wears the bat-symbol on her costume.

Batgirl's belt contains multiple supplies and gadgets.

VITAL STATS

REAL NAME Stephanie Brown
OCCUPATION Hero
HEIGHT 5ft 5in
WEIGHT 142 lbs
BASE Gotham City
ALLIES Batman, Oracle
FOES Roxy Rocket, Clarion

POWERS: Batgirl has been trained in martial arts, acrobatics, and street fighting. Her suit is lined with Kevlar to protect her against fire and electric shocks. She also has an array of gadgets at her disposal, including a collapsible bo staff, grappling hook, and Batarangs similar to those used by Batman.

SPOILER
In a previous heroic identity as the Spoiler, Stephanie often crossed paths with Tim Drake, now known as Red Robin. At first Tim felt Spoiler was a bit young and inexperienced, but the heroic pair soon developed a crush on one another.

BATMAN
THE DARK KNIGHT

When young Bruce Wayne's parents were killed, he vowed to avenge their deaths as Batman. Also known as the Dark Knight, Batman often works from the shadows, and many people believe he is just a legend. Along with his sidekick, Robin, Batman fights tirelessly to keep Gotham City's streets free of crime.

Batman's cape is lined with protective Kevlar.

VITAL STATS
REAL NAME Bruce Wayne
OCCUPATION Hero
HEIGHT 6ft 2in
WEIGHT 210 lbs
BASE Gotham City
ALLIES Robin, Batgirl, Justice League of America
FOES The Joker, Two-Face, The Penguin

He keeps all of his weapons in his utility belt.

WELCOME TO THE BATCAVE
The Batcave is a secret cave located beneath Batman's home, Wayne Manor. It houses a range of equipment and technology as well as trophies from Batman's adventures. Among his keepsakes are the Joker's playing card, a robot dinosaur, and a giant penny.

POWERS: Batman is a master detective and one of the smartest men on the planet. He is also a skilled martial artist and is proficient in many different forms of hand-to-hand combat. Batman has created many bat-themed devices that he uses in his fight against crime, such as the Batarang and the Batcomputer.

BATWOMAN

AGILE AVENGER

Batwoman is the daring new hero taking on crime and corruption in Gotham City. During the day, she is socialite Kate Kane, but when night falls she dons her cowl, ready for action. Batwoman is aided by her father, a former Marine, who helps her track criminals across the city.

Like the Dark Knight himself, Batwoman wears a high-tech utility belt.

VITAL STATS

REAL NAME Katherine "Kate" Kane

OCCUPATION Hero

HEIGHT 5ft 11in

WEIGHT 145 lbs

BASE Gotham City

ALLIES Batman, The Question

FOES Intergang, Cult of Cain

POWERS: Batwoman is a very skilled fighter and proficient acrobat, having studied many forms of martial arts. She wears a cape that enables her to glide for short distances. Batwoman also keeps an arsenal of weapons and gadgetry in her utility belt, including grappling hooks and computer trackers.

TRAIN TO WIN

Batwoman pushes herself night and day to be the best she can possibly be. She pursues criminals with a relentless drive, and trains intensely to keep up her fitness. Though she's only rarely worked with Batman, the Dark Knight has given Batwoman his seal of approval.

BEAST BOY
CHANGELING CHALLENGER

Treatment for a rare tropical disease gave Gar Logan green skin and the ability to morph into any animal. As Beast Boy, he has turned his misfortune into a career as a hero. He may crack jokes on the battlefield, but Beast Boy is serious about his role. To his teammates, he is the heart and soul of the Teen Titans.

When in animal form, Beast Boy is still able to speak and think like a human.

Green skin is a side effect of treatment for a rare disease called Sakutia.

VITAL STATS
REAL NAME Garfield "Gar" Logan
OCCUPATION Hero
HEIGHT 5ft 8in
WEIGHT 150 lbs
BASE San Francisco
ALLIES Teen Titans, Doom Patrol
FOES Fearsome Five, Brother Blood

CONTROLLING THE BEAST
Beast Boy is normally a fun-loving party guy, but in his animal form he can develop a ferocious streak when his friends are in danger. Thankfully, his fellow Teen Titans have always been able to bring Beast Boy back from the brink before he loses control completely.

POWERS: Beast Boy can change his shape into that of any beast he can imagine—even extinct animals like dinosaurs. He often has fun with his gifts, and has been known to torment his teammates as a monkey. In his human form, Beast Boy is a good fighter but prefers to defend himself with his charm and wit.

JVSTINIANO 99

Barda's Mega-Rod generates powerful energy bolts that can stun her enemies.

BIG BARDA
FIERCE FURY

Big Barda is a fierce warrior and a member of the alien race known as the New Gods. Though she's now a hero, Barda was trained in battle by the evil Granny Goodness and her Female Furies, Darkseid's elite fighting force. Barda chose to defy Granny and fight for freedom alongside her husband, Mister Miracle.

VITAL STATS
REAL NAME Barda Free
OCCUPATION New God, Hero
HEIGHT 6ft 2in
WEIGHT 217 lbs
BASE New Genesis
ALLIES Justice League of America
FOES Darkseid, Female Furies

Barda's indestructible armor enhances her already immense strength.

POWERS: Big Barda is one of the best hand-to-hand fighters in the universe. She carries with her a Mega-Rod, a weapon that is capable of intense energy blasts as well as giving its user the power of flight. Barda's indestructible armor was forged in the fires of Apokolips, her home planet.

FIGHT FOR THE FUTURE
Having been raised as a Female Fury of Apokolips, Barda never shies away from a fight. During her time with the Justice League, Barda used her fierce training to go head-to-head with a threat from one million years in the future—the Wonder Woman of the year 85,271!

BIZARRO
TWISTED TERROR

Bizarro is an imperfect copy of Superman. He was created by Lex Luthor to destroy the Man of Steel, but has not succeeded in doing so. Though he has all of Superman's amazing abilities, Bizarro is very simple-minded. He can be either childlike or brutish, and is also known for his dangerous temper tantrums.

VITAL STATS

REAL NAME None
OCCUPATION Villain
HEIGHT 6ft 3in
WEIGHT 225 lbs
BASE Mobile, Bizarro World
ALLIES Injustice League
FOES Darkseid, Female Furies

Bizarro talks in a mixed up language.

He can create duplicates of himself from his own body.

Bizarro doesn't need to eat, drink, or sleep to survive.

BIZARRO FRIENDS
Bizarro has often felt lonely. He once tried to solve this problem by creating his own cube-shaped planet called Bizarro World. Using his strange powers of self-replication, Bizarro populated his new home with twisted versions of Lois Lane and the JLA.

POWERS: Some of Bizarro's powers are the exact opposite of Superman's. Superman has heat vision while Bizarro has freezing vision; Superman has freezing breath while Bizarro has fire breath. However, both share the same incredible levels of strength and both are virtually indestructible.

BLACK ADAM
FALLEN MARVEL

Black Adam wears a lightning bolt similar to Captain Marvel's.

Black Adam was once a brave warrior in ancient Egypt, and was chosen by the wizard Shazam to receive the power of the gods. Adam's temperament made him unworthy, and he became corrupted over time, choosing a path of villainy. In modern times, Adam has tried reforming, to no avail.

VITAL STATS
REAL NAME Teth-Adam
OCCUPATION Conqueror
HEIGHT 6ft
WEIGHT 198 lbs
BASE Kahndaq
ALLIES Secret Society
FOES Justice Society of America

Black Adam is the ruler of a country named Kahndaq.

POWERS: Black Adam is powered by the Egyptian gods. Shu grants him stamina; Heru, swiftness; Amon, strength; Zehuti, wisdom; Aton, power; and Mehan, courage. Adam can fly and is almost indestructible. He is jealous that he must share the same magical power that gives Captain Marvel his abilities.

WORLD WAR THREE
Black Adam was searching for the Four Horsemen of the Apocalypse. Believing that they were hiding in the country of Bialya, he launched himself on a wild rampage that destroyed the whole nation. It took Earth's heroes a week to take the villain down in a battle that became known as World War Three.

BLACK CANARY
SONIC SIREN

Dinah Lance fights crime as the Black Canary, just like her mother before her. Dinah was a natural to take over the role, being spirited yet level-headed. Black Canary is currently one of the Birds of Prey, and is sent on missions all over the world by Oracle, who helps guide her through the toughest situations.

She keeps in contact with Oracle via circuitry embedded in her costume.

VITAL STATS

REAL NAME Dinah Laurel Lance
OCCUPATION Hero
HEIGHT 5ft 5in
WEIGHT 124 lbs
BASE Gotham City, Mobile
ALLIES Justice League of America, Birds of Prey
FOES Lady Shiva, Cheshire

Black Canary learned many of her fighting skills from the assassin Lady Shiva.

BIRDS OF PREY
When serious injuries left the hero Oracle unable to walk, she invited the daring Black Canary to be her partner in the field. Together they became the Birds of Prey. Huntress, Lady Blackhawk, and Hawk and Dove have since joined this covert group in their quest for justice.

POWERS: Black Canary is an expert in various martial arts. She is one of the best fighters on Earth and has trained with many different masters, including Batman and Wildcat. Her unique power is the canary cry, a high-pitched sound that can shatter objects and disorient anyone that hears it.

BLACK HAND
DEATH'S COLD GRIP

Black Hand's energy wand can steal and store the power from a Green Lantern's ring.

William Hand was obsessed with death. After stealing an energy-absorbing device, he became obsessed with Green Lantern, too, and used the device to torment him. He had become the Black Hand! Dark god Nekron later granted Black Hand even greater power as a member of the sinister Black Lantern Corps, and he went on to become the embodiment of death itself.

VITAL STATS
REAL NAME William Hand
OCCUPATION Villain
HEIGHT 5ft 8in
WEIGHT 140 lbs
BASE Mobile
ALLIES Black Lantern Corps
FOES Green Lantern

He gained his death touch after aliens abducted and experimented on him.

POWERS: Black Hand has a death touch—his body drains the life force from humans, animals, and plants around him. He uses an energy wand that can disrupt the power from a Green Lantern's ring. On joining the Black Lantern Corps he received a Black Lantern ring, and uses its energy to raise the dead.

DARK SPIRIT
The villain Atrocitus once came to Earth looking for William Hand. He thought that Hand was a dark spirit whom he could use for his own ends. But young William got away, taking a strange weapon dropped by Atrocitus. As Black Hand, he'd later use the weapon against the heroic Green Lanterns.

BLACK LIGHTNING
ELECTRIC ACE

As a teacher, Jefferson Pierce uses his street smarts and intelligence to help his students excel both in and out of the classroom. As Black Lightning, he uses his electrical powers to protect Metropolis. His fellow heroes in the Outsiders know they can trust him without question.

VITAL STATS

REAL NAME Jefferson Pierce

OCCUPATION Teacher, Hero

HEIGHT 6ft 1in

WEIGHT 182 lbs

BASE Metropolis

ALLIES The Outsiders, Batman

FOES Tobias Whale, Masters of Disguise

The lightning bolts he produces are powerful enough to stun his enemies.

Black Lightning trains hard to stay in peak physical condition.

He once used a special belt to control his powers, but he no longer needs it.

LIGHTNING
Black Lightning's daughter Jennifer has abilities similar to his, and serves in the Justice Society as the hero Lightning. There is a downside to Lightning's powers—her body disrupts any electrical equipment she comes into contact with. It causes her a lot of problems in her day-to-day life.

POWERS: Black Lightning is able to generate intense bolts of electricity from his fingertips. His powers are potentially devastating, and he wears a specially designed suit that helps him to control them. He's also an Olympic-level athlete and fighter, having been trained by Batman.

BLACK MANTA
MARINE MARAUDER

Black Manta's wrist gauntlets fire electric blasts.

Black Manta is the menacing and devious arch enemy of Aquaman. Not much is known about him except that he wants to dominate the ocean and he will not hesitate to demolish anyone who stands in his way. Black Manta's anger is targeted at the King of the Seas, whom he has vowed to destroy.

VITAL STATS

REAL NAME Unrevealed
OCCUPATION Villain
HEIGHT 6ft 4in
WEIGHT 250 lbs
BASE Devil's Deep
ALLIES Ocean Master, Secret Society
FOES Aquaman, Aqualad

His wetsuit adapts to underwater temperatures and pressures.

POWERS: Black Manta is an above-average fighter who also has slightly above-average strength. He wears a special wetsuit that protects him from harm, and the red lenses on his helmet are capable of firing energy blasts. He also carries a weapon that he uses to fire bolts of energy.

DANGER IN THE DEPTHS
As a young boy, Black Manta was without friends and family, adrift in the world. He became obsessed with Aquaman and envious of his power as the leader of Atlantis. Black Manta decided that one day he'd seize that power for himself—by force if necessary.

BLUE BEETLE
INSECTOID PROTECTOR

Teenager Jaime Reyes lived a quiet life in El Paso, Texas, until the day he found an alien device. The insect-shaped artifact transformed him overnight into the amazing Blue Beetle! Jaime got a crash course in how to be a hero when he teamed up with the Justice League to battle the evil Maxwell Lord.

VITAL STATS
REAL NAME Jaime Reyes
OCCUPATION High School Student, Hero
HEIGHT 5ft 8in
WEIGHT 145 lbs
BASE El Paso
ALLIES Ocean Master, Secret Society
FOES La Dama, Eclipso

Blue Beetle's metal suit can grow wings for flight.

Jaime's transformation came about when the scarab bonded to his spine while he slept.

ALIEN ARSENAL
The Blue Beetle armor can generate an array of high-powered weapons for Jaime to use in battle. Jaime is still learning to control his newfound abilities, but he's lucky to have heroic mentors in the Justice League and the Teen Titans.

POWERS: Blue Beetle's powers come from a beetle-shaped device called a scarab which fell to Earth from space. When danger threatens, the scarab emerges from Jaime's spine and encases him in a suit of indestructible metal armor. The armor also generates weapons and allows Jaime to fly and shoot laser beams.

BLUE DEVIL
GALLANT GOBLIN

His weapon of choice is a power staff which he uses to fire bolts of energy.

Blue Devil's horns give him a devilish appearance.

Dan Cassidy was desperate to find fame as an actor and was willing to do anything to achieve it. One day he was tricked into selling his soul to a demon, who promised him success but then turned him into the Blue Devil. Dan swore to defy the demon and fight against the darkness, and has since become a hero.

VITAL STATS

REAL NAME Daniel Patrick Cassidy

OCCUPATION Demon, Hero

HEIGHT 6ft 8in

WEIGHT 365 lbs

BASE Mobile

ALLIES Shadowpact

FOES Nebiros, Neron

POWERS: Blue Devil is incredibly strong and he has a healing factor that enables his body to repair itself quickly. He has enhanced speed and acute senses, and has mastered multiple forms of martial arts. Blue Devil is currently a member of the team of magically-powered heroes known as the Shadowpact.

KID DEVIL
Eddie Bloomberg met Blue Devil on a movie set and became his number one fan. Though Blue Devil didn't want a sidekick, Eddie became Kid Devil, hoping to impress him. While Kid Devil never became Blue Devil's official sidekick, he later joined the Teen Titans as Red Devil.

31

BOOSTER GOLD

FUTURISTIC HERO

Booster Gold came from the future with one goal in mind: to be rich and famous. Before long, though, he found himself becoming a hero—and liked it! Booster teamed up with time-traveler Rip Hunter and together they protect all of history, preventing bad guys from changing the past.

VITAL STATS

REAL NAME Michael Jon Carter

OCCUPATION Time Traveler, Hero

HEIGHT 6ft 5in

WEIGHT 215 lbs

BASE Mobile

ALLIES Rip Hunter, Blue Beetle

FOES Mister Mind, Black Beetle

Wrist gauntlets contain the main controls for Booster's suit.

He stole his Legion flight ring from a 25th century museum.

Booster has a flying robot companion named Skeets.

RIP HUNTER, TIME MASTER

Experienced time traveler Rip Hunter serves as Booster Gold's mentor and together they travel the time stream in their amazing Time Sphere. Their relationship can be strained, and Hunter keeps a secret from Booster—he's actually Booster's son from the future.

POWERS: Booster Gold's suit is encased in a protective force field that shields him from harm. He wears a Legion flight ring that allows him to fly. He can also shoot lasers from his wrist gauntlets. Booster is a good fighter but prefers using his charm and bravado in tough situations.

BRAINIAC
CYBER CONQUEROR

His high-tech suit allows him to connect directly to his ship.

Brainiac is a cold-hearted alien being who is obsessed with knowledge. For centuries he has roamed the universe, looking for new additions to his collection of shrunken, bottled cities. Brainiac once set his sights on Metropolis but was defeated by Superman, who restored the city to its normal size.

Brainiac has created many different versions of himself to trick people.

VITAL STATS
REAL NAME Vril Dox
OCCUPATION Cyber Conqueror
HEIGHT Variable
WEIGHT Variable
BASE Mobile
ALLIES Lex Luthor
FOES Superman

SKULL SHIP
As he travels the universe looking for civilizations to conquer, Brainiac protects his treasures deep within his skull-shaped spaceship. Brainiac himself is connected to the ship's core, and can quickly download information about planets he wishes to destroy.

POWERS: Brainiac is one of the most intelligent beings in the galaxy, with a 12th level intellect (humans function at only 6th level). He can fight quite well, but prefers to defend himself in his skull-shaped spaceship with its protective weaponry. Brainiac's cold, calculating behavior makes him a serious threat to the universe.

BRAINIAC 5
ALIEN GENIUS

Brainiac 5 is a member of the Legion of Super-Heroes and is considered one of the smartest people in the universe. Although he can be contrary at times, Brainiac 5 remains one of the most devoted Legionnaires. His brilliant mind has made him able to solve some of the team's most difficult problems.

VITAL STATS
REAL NAME Querl Dox
OCCUPATION Scientist, Legionnaire
HEIGHT 5ft 7in
WEIGHT 135 lbs
BASE Colu, 31st century Earth
ALLIES Legion of Super-Heroes
FOES Dominators

Like everyone from the planet Colu, Brainiac 5 has green skin.

He sometimes lacks patience when communicating with less intelligent beings.

FORCE FIELD BELT
Among Brainiac 5's many brilliant inventions, his force field belt stands out as the most ingenious. The belt controls a force field so powerful that almost nothing can penetrate it. Brainiac 5 uses the force field to surround and protect himself, and it can also be used to trap his enemies.

POWERS: Brainiac 5 is a 12th level intellect, and thus a super-genius. He's brilliant at calculations as well as deductive reasoning. He also has an amazing memory and exceptional technical knowledge. Brainiac 5 uses a force field to shield himself from danger and is an average hand-to-hand fighter.

CAPTAIN ATOM
NUCLEAR SOLDIER

His extensive army training has made him an expert military tactician.

Captain Atom is a nuclear-powered solider and a proud member of the Justice League. His devastating energy blasts have helped the team to defeat many foes. Atom sometimes suffers an energy overload and is transported to the future, where he struggles to find his way home.

VITAL STATS

REAL NAME Nathaniel "Nate" Adam

OCCUPATION Army Captain, Hero

HEIGHT 6ft 4in

WEIGHT 200 lbs

BASE Mobile

ALLIES Justice League of America, Superman

FOES Major Force, Plastique

Captain Atom is encased in an unbreakable metal skin.

RISE OF MONARCH
A suit of experimental armor spelled trouble for Captain Atom. Wearing it, he was bounced around a multitude of parallel universes and left with a fragmented mind. No longer his heroic self, he became the villain Monarch and led a rebellion against the Monitors.

POWERS: Captain Atom's body is encased in an alien metal that gives him super-strength and the ability to fly and fire bolts of atomic energy. He can also absorb energy from outside his body and manipulate it, but if he absorbs too much he will explode. Atom's army training makes him an expert fighter.

CAPTAIN BOOMERANG

BACKFIRE BRIGAND

Captain Boomerang is a ruthless thief and a member of the Flash's Rogues Gallery of enemies. He's an expert marksman with a sharp tongue, and he never shies away from trouble. Captain Boomerang was recently given a chance to start a new life, but he still chose to pursue a career in crime.

VITAL STATS

REAL NAME George "Digger" Harkness

OCCUPATION Criminal

HEIGHT 5ft 9in

WEIGHT 167 lbs

BASE Keystone City

ALLIES The Rogues

FOES The Flash

His suit is equipped with a variety of specially-made boomerangs.

HARSH CHILDHOOD

Digger Harkness was raised in Australia in a life of poverty. His abusive father paid him no attention, so the boy took to making boomerangs to pass the time. After becoming an expert boomerang thrower, Digger embarked on a life of villainy using his favorite weapon.

POWERS: Captain Boomerang is an expert with boomerangs and has created a variety of them, each with its own special power. These include explosive, electrified, and bladed boomerangs. Aside from his skill with his namesake weapons, Boomerang is an average fighter and hand-to-hand combatant.

CAPTAIN COLD

FROSTY FELON

Captain Cold invented his freezing gun so he could create traps made of ice.

Lenny Snart became fascinated with ice when he was a little boy riding in his grandfather's ice cream truck. As an adult, he chose a life of villainy, and naturally decided to give it an icy twist! Now the leader of the Flash's Rogues Gallery, Captain Cold is always planning his next big robbery.

VITAL STATS

REAL NAME Leonard "Lenny" Snart
OCCUPATION Criminal
HEIGHT 6ft 2in
WEIGHT 196 lbs
BASE Central City, Keystone City
ALLIES The Rogues
FOES The Flash

Despite his love of frosty weather, Cold keeps himself warm in a protective suit.

POWERS: Captain Cold carries two cold-guns, which he uses to create various ice-related traps and weapons. His guns can imprison people in blocks of ice as well as create dangerous slicks. Cold wears special goggles to protect his eyes from the bright flash given off by his guns.

GOLDEN GLIDER
Captain Cold's sister, Lisa, followed in his criminal footsteps, becoming the ice-skating villain called Golden Glider. Lisa was betrayed by a partner and murdered with Captain Cold's own freezing gun. Cold was left in pieces and has vowed to avenge his sister's death.

CAPTAIN MARVEL
THE WORLD'S MIGHTIEST MORTAL

Young Billy Batson was given magical powers by an ancient wizard. Now, whenever he utters the word "Shazam!" he becomes Captain Marvel, champion of justice. The transformation from pint-sized teen to fully fledged super hero is a dramatic one, but Billy's youthful idealism is unchanged.

VITAL STATS

REAL NAME William Joseph "Billy" Batson

OCCUPATION Radio Host, Hero

HEIGHT (as Billy) 5ft 4in, (as Marvel) 6ft 2in

WEIGHT (as Billy) 110 lbs, (as Marvel) 215 lbs

BASE Fawcett City

ALLIES Justice Society of America

FOES Black Adam

Billy Batson is changed into Captain Marvel by a bolt of mystical lightning.

Captain Marvel uses his golden gauntlets to shield himself.

HEROES UNITE
Marvel shares the power of Shazam with his younger sister, Mary Marvel. His friend, Freddy Freeman, can also harness these powers when he utters the name "Captain Marvel!" The trio of heroes often join forces, lending each other extra power when needed.

POWERS: Captain Marvel is powered by ancient gods and legendary figures. The magic word—Shazam—comes from their initials. Solomon grants him wisdom; Hercules, strength; Atlas, stamina; Zeus, power; Achilles, courage; and Mercury, speed. Captain Marvel can also fly and is virtually indestructible.

CATWOMAN
FELINE FEMME FATALE

Catwoman's goggles protect her eyes and help her to see at night.

Catwoman is a master thief and cat burglar who prowls the rooftops of Gotham City looking for her next big catch. Though she may be a criminal, Catwoman has always had an uneasy friendship with Batman. She is one of the few people who know his identity, and has even aided him on several cases.

VITAL STATS

REAL NAME Selina Kyle
OCCUPATION Thief, Vigilante
HEIGHT 5ft 7in
WEIGHT 133 lbs
BASE Gotham City
ALLIES Poison Ivy, Harley Quinn
FOES Batman, Robin

Her suit has razor-sharp claws which she uses to climb walls.

FORBIDDEN LOVE
Catwoman straddles the line between hero and villain. She is fiercely protective of the East End of Gotham City and has vowed to protect it. But she has also manipulated Batman, using her charms to evade capture, and even convincing the Dark Knight that he had feelings for her.

POWERS: Catwoman is an Olympic-level acrobat and has learned many different fighting techniques. She's studied boxing with Wildcat and street fighting with investigator Slam Bradley. She's even picked up some detective tricks from Batman over the years. The bullwhip and cat o' nine tails are her weapons of choice.

CHEETAH
CLAWS OF EVIL

Treasure hunter Barbara Minerva discovered a secret temple in Africa. After agreeing to take part in an ancient ritual there, she became the ferocious and cunning Cheetah. An enemy of Wonder Woman, Cheetah often teams up with like-minded villains in the hope that together they'll be able to defeat her.

VITAL STATS

REAL NAME Barbara Ann Minerva

OCCUPATION Villain, Archaeologist

HEIGHT 5ft 9in

WEIGHT 140 lbs

BASE Mobile

ALLIES Doctor Psycho, Giganta

FOES Wonder Woman

> Cheetah uses her prehensile tail to grasp objects as weapons.

> Cheetah uses her sharpened claws and teeth to attack her prey.

SEBASTIAN BALLESTEROS
Argentinian businessman Sebastian Ballesteros once stole the power of Urzkartaga from Barbara Minerva and became the new, male Cheetah. After a bitter power struggle, Barbara was able to destroy Ballesteros and return the power to her own body.

POWERS: Cheetah's power comes from an ancient plant-god called Urzkartaga. When possessed by the god, her body is transformed into a cheetah-like form and she gains above-average strength, speed, and agility. In her other identity as Barbara Minerva, she is highly intelligent, but possesses no fighting skills.

CHEMO
FORMULA FOR DESTRUCTION

Chemo is one of the most dangerous creatures on the planet. His giant body houses a cocktail of deadly chemicals that could spell disaster for anyone in his path. At one time, Lex Luthor's company, LexCorp, used traces of chemicals taken from Chemo to create a number of smaller "baby" Chemos.

Chemo spews toxic green acid from his mouth.

Chemo can grow to 100 feet.

VITAL STATS

REAL NAME Chemo
OCCUPATION Villain
HEIGHT 25ft–100ft
WEIGHT 5,000 lbs–90,000 lbs
BASE Mobile
ALLIES Secret Society of Super-Villains
FOES Metal Men

BLÜDHAVEN'S DESTRUCTION
The Secret Society of Super-Villains once used Chemo as a toxic bomb. They dropped him on the city of Blüdhaven, destroying it and contaminating nearby areas. When Chemo tried to regenerate, Superman flung the poison-filled villain into space where he could do no harm.

POWERS: Chemo's outer shell is made of an indestructible plastic. Inside is a toxic mix of chemicals that have mutated over time, bringing him to life. Chemo can control his size and has superhuman endurance and strength. He's also invulnerable to attack, though his large frame makes his movements quite cumbersome.

CHESHIRE
DEADLY BEAUTY

Cheshire is a beautiful but dangerous terrorist and assassin. Her only true loyalty is to herself, and she will betray even her closest friends in order to get what she wants. She is a member of the Secret Society of Super-Villains but because of her devious ways, even her own teammates rarely trust her.

VITAL STATS

REAL NAME Jade Nguyen
OCCUPATION Villain
HEIGHT 5ft 9in
WEIGHT 141 lbs
BASE Mobile
ALLIES Secret Society of Super-Villains
FOES Titans

Cheshire's razor sharp fingertips are dipped in poison.

SECOND CHANCES
Cheshire was recently drafted by the assassin Deathstroke to be a part of his new team of villains-for-hire. He believes that Cheshire has lost her dangerous edge, so he's given her a new opportunity to regain it. Cheshire, however, doesn't trust Deathstroke.

POWERS: Cheshire is a triple-jointed acrobat and a superior hand-to-hand combatant. She has trained extensively in many fighting styles. Cheshire uses a variety of weapons in battle and is known to be an expert in deadly poisons. She often dips her weapons in various concoctions to give them a poisonous edge.

CIRCE
DIABOLICAL DIVA

Circe is an evil witch who sold her soul to the goddess Hecate in exchange for magical powers. Over the years, Circe has taken many forms, and often disguises herself in order to trick people into obeying her. Circe is the sworn enemy of Wonder Woman, whose role as a peacemaker she despises.

Circe uses her attractiveness to lure men into her traps.

She uses ancient flowers and herbs to conjure her wicked spells.

VITAL STATS
REAL NAME Circe
OCCUPATION Sorceress
HEIGHT 5ft 11in
WEIGHT 145 lbs
BASE Mobile
ALLIES Injustice League
FOES Wonder Woman

MANIMAL
As a member of Lex Luthor's Injustice Gang, Circe once faced off against Plastic Man, magically turning him into a pig. However, because of Plastic Man's ability to shape-shift, the stretchable hero easily wiggled out of Circe's spell.

POWERS: Circe is a powerful sorceress. Her ancient magic can turn men into animals called "bestiamorphs." Her magic also allows her to alter her appearance, taking any form she chooses. While she is not a strong fighter, Circe can defend herself with bolts of energy which she shoots from her hands.

CLAYFACE
MUD MONSTER

Many criminals have taken on the identity of Clayface over the years, each more powerful than the last. They've gotten Batman into some sticky situations, and some have even fought him together as the Mudpack. The most recent Clayface is a former actor who seeks revenge on those who betrayed him.

VITAL STATS
REAL NAME Basil Karlo
OCCUPATION Villain
HEIGHT 5ft 11in
WEIGHT 178 lbs
BASE Gotham City
ALLIES Mudpack, Secret Society of Super-Villains
FOES Batman

His weakness is extreme cold.

Clayface's mud-like body can morph into any shape.

MUDPACK
The Mudpack is made up of various criminals who have been known as Clayface over the years, including treasure hunter Matt Hagen, scientist Preston Payne, and terrorist Sondra Fuller. Basil Karlo injected himself with samples of his clay colleagues, making him the ultimate Clayface.

POWERS: Clayface's body is made entirely of chemically altered clay, which allows him to change his shape, size, and density. He can also regenerate damaged parts of his body. Karlo uses his acting experience to impersonate people as Clayface. He possesses superhuman strength and is incredibly agile.

CONGORILLA
AMAZING APE

Thick, tough skin protects Congorilla during a fight.

Congo Bill was an explorer who settled in Africa. There, a dying chieftain gave him a magic ring that allowed him to switch bodies with the great Golden Gorilla of the jungle. When Bill's human body died, he became trapped in his ape body and now, as Congorilla, he fights alongside the Justice League of America.

VITAL STATS

REAL NAME Congo Bill
OCCUPATION Adventurer
HEIGHT 6ft 8in
WEIGHT 706 lbs
BASE Mobile
ALLIES Justice League of America, Forgotten Heroes
FOES Prometheus

Congorilla can grow in size depending on his mood.

POWERS: Congorilla is the rare Golden Gorilla of legend. He is extremely intelligent, having retained all the knowledge and intellect of Congo Bill. His huge gorilla body gives him super-strength and agility, and he is an excellent tracker. Recently, it was revealed that Congorilla's body can grow in size.

CONGO BILL
Shortly after receiving his magical ring, Bill became trapped in a cave. To save his life, he rubbed the ring, transferring his consciousness into the body of the Golden Gorilla. At the same time, the Gorilla's mind was transferred into Bill's body.

COSMIC BOY
MASTER OF MAGNETISM

Cosmic Boy is a hero with a magnetic personality and a cool head. As a co-founder of the Legion of Super-Heroes, he must often make tough choices to protect his teammates. Cosmic Boy lives in the 31st century, but once went back in time to recruit young Clark Kent before he became Superman.

VITAL STATS

REAL NAME Rokk Krinn
OCCUPATION Legionnaire
HEIGHT 6ft
WEIGHT 190 lbs
BASE 31st century Earth
ALLIES Legion of Super-Heroes
FOES Cosmic King

He can manipulate the metal discs on his costume for use as weapons.

A magnetic pulse from Cosmic Boy packs a mighty force.

SUPER FRIEND
Brainiac 5 created a Time Bubble in case the Legion needed to travel through time. On its maiden voyage, Cosmic Boy, Lightning Lad, and Saturn Girl visited 20th century Smallville to recruit young Clark Kent. They considered him to be the greatest hero of that era.

POWERS: Cosmic Boy is from the planet Braal and like everyone on his world, he has the power to control magnetic forces. He can attract, repel, or manipulate any objects that are made of metal or contain metal. Cosmic Boy uses his Legion flight ring to fly during battle.

The Creeper is known for his howling cackle.

THE CREEPER
WEIRD AND WILD

During the day, Jack Ryder is a television reporter who will do anything for a story. At night, he magically transforms himself into the Creeper—a wild-eyed, freakish vigilante. When Ryder becomes the Creeper, his frightening appearance and insane behavior scares criminals into confessing their crimes.

The Creeper costume gives Jack Ryder bright yellow skin and tufts of red fur.

VITAL STATS
REAL NAME Jack Ryder
OCCUPATION Reporter, Adventurer
HEIGHT 6ft
WEIGHT 194 lbs
BASE Mobile
ALLIES The Outsiders
FOES Eclipso

POWERS: Jack Ryder is bonded with the Creeper costume, and can transform himself at will. The transformations take their toll on his mental stability and often leave him exhausted when he returns to normal. The Creeper has used his amazing strength, stamina, and agility to develop his own ferocious fighting style.

FRICTION
The Creeper and Batman have had a very complicated relationship. At first the Dark Knight didn't know whether the yellow-skinned wild child was a servant of good or evil. That all changed when the Creeper helped to clear Batman's name during an important case.

47

CRIME SYNDICATE
THE ANTI-JUSTICE LEAGUE

The Crime Syndicate is a twisted version of the Justice League from a parallel universe of evil. On its anti-matter world, evil wins and good is a distant memory. The Crime Syndicate often travels to our Earth for sport, but its members' greed and mistrust of one another usually leads to their downfall.

MEMBERS INCLUDE

1 SUPERWOMAN Superwoman is an Amazon who enjoys pitting Ultraman and Owlman against one another.

2 OWLMAN Owlman plots to destroy the world (and sometimes his own teammates, too).

3 POWER RING An ancient entity called Volthoom gives Power Ring the ability to create yellow energy constructs.

4 ULTRAMAN Team leader Ultraman is an astronaut who was experimented on by aliens.

5 JOHNNY QUICK "Speed Juice" gives Johnny Quick the power to run and fight at incredible velocities.

EVIL EARTHS
Another universe has a *different* villainous twist. On Earth-3, the evil Crime Society is kept at bay by the heroic Riddler Family, whose members include Three-Face, Harlequin, and the Riddler, himself!

CRIMSON AVENGER

VICIOUS VIGILANTE

Crimson Avenger's magical guns don't have a trigger.

Crimson Avenger is a mysterious vigilante who uses two magic guns to bring criminals to justice. She's a woman of few words and relies on her actions to speak for her. Crimson's eyes are hidden by a blindfold, and her identity remains a mystery that even the Justice Society has been unable to solve.

VITAL STATS

REAL NAME Unknown
OCCUPATION Vigilante
HEIGHT 5ft 8in
WEIGHT 136 lbs
BASE Mobile
ALLIES Justice Society of America
FOES Ultra-Humanite

Her chest insignia symbolizes the violence she's fated to avenge.

Crimson Avenger always appears out of a mysterious red mist.

POWERS: Crimson Avenger carries two identical pistols that fire magical bullets and never need to be reloaded. Not much is known about her. It has been revealed that Crimson's supernatural guns were given to her so that she could avenge the deaths of others. The guns are also rumored to be cursed.

THE FIRST SUPER HERO

Young publisher Lee Travis felt a higher calling, so he donned a hat and cloak in the name of justice and became the original Crimson Avenger. Considered to be the first ever super hero, Crimson Avenger joined the Seven Soldiers of Victory and fought during World War II.

CYBORG
METAL MAN

Victor Stone was an athlete with a bright future, until an accident at his father's laboratory injured him. In order to save his son, Victor's father created experimental cybernetic parts that gave Vic special abilities. Despite his astonishing gifts, Cyborg sometimes feels as if his metal body is a prison.

VITAL STATS

REAL NAME Victor Stone
OCCUPATION Hero
HEIGHT 6ft 6in
WEIGHT 340 lbs
BASE Mobile
ALLIES Teen Titans, Justice League of America
FOES Fearsome Five

Parts of Cyborg's body are made of impenetrable metal.

Cyborg has various laser devices attached to his wrist gauntlets.

ALIEN UPGRADE
When Cyborg's body was upgraded by the alien Technis he became a cold, emotionless robot. Beast Boy helped him regain his humanity by placing him inside a suit called the Omegadrome, which turned him gold and allowed him to morph into a variety of weapons.

POWERS: Cyborg's cybernetic body protects him from harm and gives him super-strength, speed, and stamina. He has many weapons at his disposal, including a sonic disruptor designed to throw his enemies off balance. Cyborg is also a brilliant scientist and skilled hand-to-hand fighter.

CYBORG SUPERMAN
BIONIC BAD GUY

His face and body are covered in frightening cybernetic circuitry.

While on a mission, astronaut Hank Henshaw was bombarded with dangerous cosmic rays that damaged his body, making him half-man, half-machine. Hank blames Superman for his condition and has vowed to destroy the Man of Steel. In the past, he has posed as Superman in an attempt to discredit him.

VITAL STATS
REAL NAME Hank Henshaw
OCCUPATION Villain
HEIGHT Variable
WEIGHT Variable
BASE Outer Space
ALLIES Mongul
FOES Superman, Green Lantern

POWERS: Cyborg Superman's body is made up of mechanical parts which he uses to control other forms of machinery. His machine parts can also transform into an array of tools and weapons, and he can regenerate any of them, making him indestructible. His cyborg body gives him incredible strength as well.

BATTLE OF THE SUPERMEN
When Superman was defeated in battle, the Cyborg Superman came forth claiming to be the Man of Steel reborn. The villain's ruse was brought to an end when the real Superman returned to try to stop the Cyborg Superman and Mongul from destroying Coast City.

CYCLONE
HEIRESS TO THE AIR

Maxine Hunkel might seem like a typical college student, but she's also Cyclone—the super-powered granddaughter of the original Red Tornado. Cyclone is a talkative, bubbly girl. She idolizes her Justice Society teammates who in turn admire her positive outlook. Together they protect the world from evil.

VITAL STATS
REAL NAME Maxine Hunkel
OCCUPATION Hero
HEIGHT 5ft 7in
WEIGHT 130 lbs
BASE New York City
ALLIES Justice Society of America
FOES T.O. Morrow

Cyclone made her costume with the help of Stargirl.

MA HUNKEL
Cyclone's grandmother, Ma Hunkel, was once the crime-fighting Red Tornado of World War II. For years, Ma was in the Witness Protection Program but the Justice Society informed her that it was safe to live free once again. She is now the caretaker of the team's museum headquarters.

POWERS: Cyclone can manipulate the winds, and create powerful bursts of air that can be used as weapons. She can also fly and control sound waves by manipulating the air currents around her. Cyclone has a thirst for knowledge and is always researching new ways to apply her developing powers.

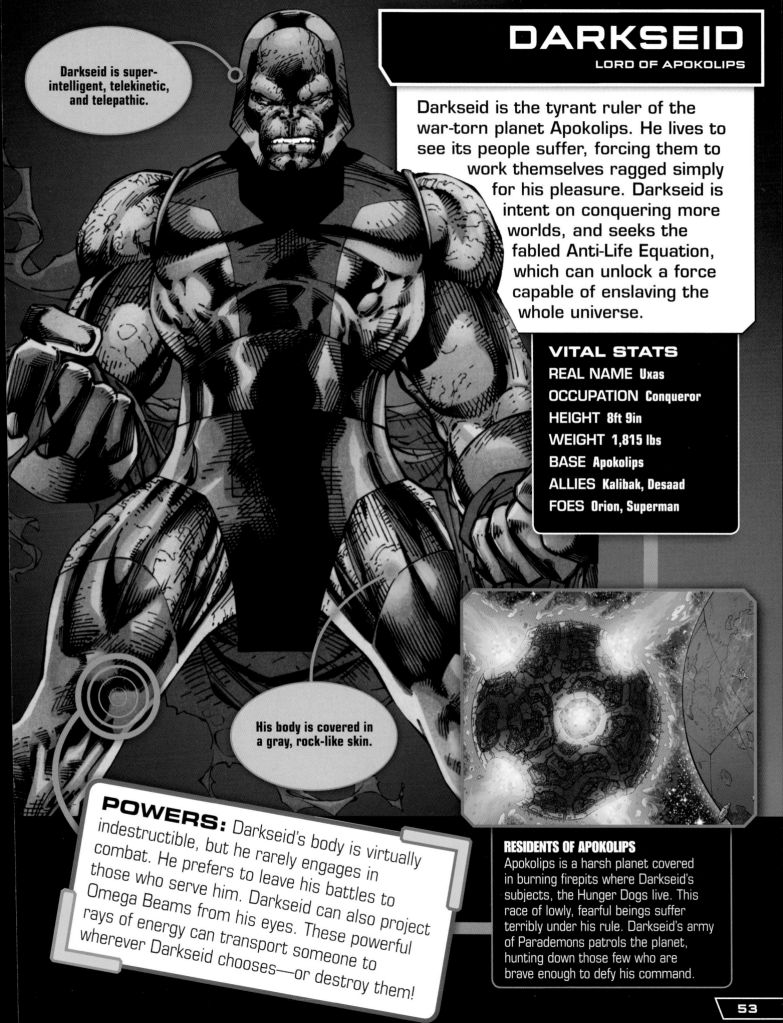

DARKSEID
LORD OF APOKOLIPS

Darkseid is super-intelligent, telekinetic, and telepathic.

Darkseid is the tyrant ruler of the war-torn planet Apokolips. He lives to see its people suffer, forcing them to work themselves ragged simply for his pleasure. Darkseid is intent on conquering more worlds, and seeks the fabled Anti-Life Equation, which can unlock a force capable of enslaving the whole universe.

VITAL STATS

REAL NAME Uxas
OCCUPATION Conqueror
HEIGHT 8ft 9in
WEIGHT 1,815 lbs
BASE Apokolips
ALLIES Kalibak, Desaad
FOES Orion, Superman

His body is covered in a gray, rock-like skin.

POWERS: Darkseid's body is virtually indestructible, but he rarely engages in combat. He prefers to leave his battles to those who serve him. Darkseid can also project Omega Beams from his eyes. These powerful rays of energy can transport someone to wherever Darkseid chooses—or destroy them!

RESIDENTS OF APOKOLIPS
Apokolips is a harsh planet covered in burning firepits where Darkseid's subjects, the Hunger Dogs live. This race of lowly, fearful beings suffer terribly under his rule. Darkseid's army of Parademons patrols the planet, hunting down those few who are brave enough to defy his command.

DEADMAN
UNSEEN HERO

Boston Brand's time as a circus acrobat was cut short the day his life was taken by a mysterious assassin. Brand's spirit lives on, however, as the ghostly Deadman. He wanders the Earth as an invisible phantom, performing heroic deeds and searching for, but never finding, the peace he craves.

VITAL STATS

REAL NAME Boston Brand

OCCUPATION Acrobat, Hero

HEIGHT 6ft

WEIGHT Inapplicable

BASE Mobile

ALLIES Sentinels of Magic, Batman

FOES League of Assassins, Asmodel

His skin is a deathly white color.

Deadman still wears his costume from his days as an acrobat.

POSSESSION
One of Deadman's favorite bodies to inhabit is that of Batman. Though Batman doesn't possess any superpowers, Deadman enjoys using the Dark Knight's agility and acrobatic skills to their fullest. It reminds him of his previous life as circus performer Boston Brand.

POWERS: Deadman's spirit can inhabit and control anyone he chooses. He's also able to use all their abilities, though in many cases he doesn't know how. Deadman possesses the White Lantern Ring of Life, which can resurrect the dead. While alive, he was an agile acrobat, Olympic-level athlete, and trained fighter.

Deadshot's mask features a sight which helps him aim.

DEADSHOT
ARMED FOR TERROR

Deadshot is the world's best marksman—there's no target this masked villain can't hit! As a young boy, Floyd Lawton saw his family ripped apart by anger and hatred. Violence was all he knew, and it turned him into a cold, heartless killer. Deadshot will hunt down anyone—for the right price.

Deadshot often uses a pair of silenced, wrist-mounted pistols.

VITAL STATS
REAL NAME Floyd Lawton
OCCUPATION Mercenary
HEIGHT 6ft 1in
WEIGHT 193 lbs
BASE Mobile
ALLIES Secret Six
FOES Batman

POWERS: Deadshot has perfect aim and can hit a target from great distances. He is not afraid of death, and will take risks that many others won't. Deadshot is also an above-average hand-to-hand fighter, and possesses knowledge of a variety of different guns. His wrist gauntlets fire small but powerful bullets.

FRIENDS AND ENEMIES
Deadshot is primarily known as a lone marksman but has recently aligned with the Secret Six—a team of criminals. Though he sticks with the team for business reasons, Deadshot often finds himself at odds with fellow member Catman, whom he considers his rival.

DEATHSTROKE
THE TERMINATOR

He was once Army Major Slade Wilson—until a secret experiment turned him into a super-soldier. The process left him unstable and now he's Deathstroke, an international assassin-for-hire. Cold, calculating, and ruthless, Deathstroke also seeks vengeance against those who have targeted his family.

VITAL STATS

REAL NAME Slade Wilson
OCCUPATION Villain
HEIGHT 6ft 4in
WEIGHT 225 lbs
BASE Mobile
ALLIES Secret Society of Super-Villains
FOES Teen Titans

Deathstroke's right eye is missing due to a gunshot wound.

Deathstroke uses both a sword and a gun in battle.

RAVAGER
When Deathstroke lost his son in battle, the villain vowed never to involve his children in his affairs again. He later went back on his vow and trained his daughter Rose to become Ravager. She soon defied her father's control, and joined the Teen Titans as a hero.

POWERS: Deathstroke can use over 90% of his brain capacity, making him incredibly intelligent and methodical. His body has been changed by the super-soldier serum, so he has superhuman strength, senses, and reflexes. Despite being blind in one eye, Deathstroke is a top fighter who can use a variety of weapons.

THE DEMON
RHYMING FIEND

The Demon's red eyes, horns, and fangs give him a frightening appearance.

When magic expert Jason Blood needs extra protection from the dangers of the mystical world, he transforms into Etrigan. Also known as the Demon, this mischievous, unpredictable creature talks in rhymes and has been bound to Blood since the days of Camelot.

VITAL STATS
REAL NAME Jason Blood, Etrigan
OCCUPATION Rhyming Demon
HEIGHT 6ft 4in
WEIGHT 352 lbs
BASE Hell
ALLIES Merlin, Batman
FOES Blue Devil, Shadowpact

JASON BLOOD
Conjuror Jason Blood is an accomplished magician even without the aid of his devilish alter-ego. When the Justice League was banished to the Obsidian Age, Blood was called upon as a reserve member of the team, where he offered his counsel on mystical affairs.

POWERS: The Demon's knowledge of magic is extensive, though he prefers to simply destroy his enemies with his flaming breath. His brutish form gives him great strength and endurance. The Demon's alter-ego, Jason Blood, is a powerful spell-caster who possesses a deep understanding of magic.

57

DESPERO
GALACTIC SLAVEMASTER

Despero is a vicious warlord from the planet Kalanor who enslaves people across the galaxy. He is a brutish fighter, and is also brilliant at playing war games. He has a deep hatred for the Justice League of America, who stand in the way of his total domination.

VITAL STATS

REAL NAME Despero

OCCUPATION Conqueror

HEIGHT 6ft 5in

WEIGHT 289 lbs

BASE Mobile

ALLIES Ultra-Humanite, Time Stealers

FOES Justice League of America

Despero's third eye can project blasts of telepathic energy.

He can use his powers to grow to enormous proportions.

DEADLY GAMES

Despero first encountered the heroes of Earth while pursuing two rebels who had escaped from Kalanor. The rebels sought safe haven with the Justice League, so Despero challenged the Flash to a game of chess to decide their fate. The Scarlet Speedster won, thwarting Despero and saving the rebels.

POWERS: Despero possesses a third eye in the middle of his forehead which he uses to hypnotize his enemies. Once under his command, his slaves will do anything he wishes. His third eye can also produce forceful energy blasts. Despero has above average strength, and an unmatched thirst for battle.

DETECTIVE CHIMP

APE OPERATIVE

Detective Chimp wears a hat similar to that of his idol, Sherlock Holmes.

Detective Chimp is a simian sleuth who fights crime as a member of the Shadowpact group. He's just as smart as a human and takes his job solving mysteries very seriously. Though Detective Chimp can be a bit cranky and stubborn, this is one detective who doesn't monkey around.

VITAL STATS

REAL NAME Bobo
OCCUPATION Detective
HEIGHT 3ft 7in
WEIGHT 76 lbs
BASE Mobile
ALLIES Shadowpact
FOES Spectre

Being an old-fashioned sleuth, he uses a magnifying glass to look for clues.

POWERS: Detective Chimp is highly intelligent and has extraordinary powers of deduction. Because he's an ape, he also possesses excellent agility and average strength. Detective Chimp has the power to communicate with all types of animals, an ability he uses often in his investigations.

SHADOWPACT

Detective Chimp was perfectly happy to solve mysteries on his own and enjoy life to the fullest—until the Spectre decided to destroy all the magic in the universe. Together with Blue Devil, Enchantress, Nightmaster, and others, Chimp formed the Shadowpact to oppose the Spectre.

DOCTOR FATE
MYSTIC MAVEN

Doctor Kent Nelson was down on his luck, and was looking for something to help him get his life back together. Suddenly a mysterious helmet appeared. Kent put it on, and was transformed into Doctor Fate, protector of Order and Chaos. Now that he's found his purpose in life, Kent makes his own luck.

VITAL STATS
REAL NAME Doctor Kent V. Nelson
OCCUPATION Sorcerer
HEIGHT 6ft
WEIGHT 180 lbs
BASE Mobile
ALLIES Justice Society of America
FOES Wotan

The helmet had many other owners before it came into Doctor Fate's possession.

Doctor Fate's golden cloak is known as the Cloak of Destiny.

FATE'S TOWER
The Tower of Fate is where Doctor Fate keeps all the magical talismans and artifacts that he's collected through the millennia. As a safe haven between realms, the inside of the tower rests in another dimension and only a select few are granted entry.

POWERS: Doctor Fate is guided by the voice of the sorcerer Nabu, whom he can hear through his mystical helmet. Though Nabu is wise, he has his own agenda and sometimes leads Doctor Fate into danger. Doctor Fate is an excellent spell-caster and can project intense energy bolts shaped like Egyptian ankhs.

DOCTOR LIGHT
LUMINARY OF EVIL

His mind was wiped clean by Zatanna after he attacked the Justice League.

Doctor Arthur Light was a scientist at S.T.A.R. Labs, a respected research facility. He craved power and chose to use his talents in the service of evil. But unfortunately for Doctor Light, his attempts at villainy failed to light up the underworld and he is often mocked by his criminal colleagues as a joke.

VITAL STATS

REAL NAME Doctor Arthur Light

OCCUPATION Villain

HEIGHT 5ft 11in

WEIGHT 171 lbs

BASE Mobile

ALLIES Secret Society of Super-Villains, Fearsome Five

FOES Justice League, Team Titans

Doctor Light's suit is able to absorb light and project it back at his enemies.

POWERS: Doctor Light's background in science helped him develop his high-tech suit which allows him to control and manipulate light in all of its forms. He's able to create hard-light energy constructs (solid objects) in any shape he imagines. Doctor Light is not a good hand-to-hand combatant, and often runs from fights.

FEARSOME FIVE
Doctor Light is a founding member of the Fearsome Five, a group of villains bent on destroying the Teen Titans. Other members of the Fearsome Five include the hulking Mammoth and his sister, Shimmer, who can transmute elements, as well as teleporter Gizmo and mental master Psimon.

DOCTOR MID-NITE
SAVIOR IN THE DARK

Shortly after being injected with an experimental drug, Doctor Pieter Cross was in an accident. He awoke to discover that he could only see in total darkness! As Doctor Mid-Nite, Pieter became an invaluable member of the Justice Society and is regarded as one of Earth's foremost super hero doctors.

His owl, Charlie, is specially trained and protects him from unseen danger.

Doctor Mid-Nite's infrared goggles help him to see.

His protective suit guards him from attack.

VITAL STATS
REAL NAME Doctor Pieter Anton Cross
OCCUPATION Doctor, Hero
HEIGHT 5ft 10in
WEIGHT 175 lbs
BASE Portsmouth City
ALLIES Justice Society of America
FOES Spirit King

MEDICAL MARVEL
Doctor Mid-Nite is often called upon to assist in the treatment of his fellow heroes, and he uses his special equipment to heal them. In addition to these services, he runs a free clinic in Portsmouth, Washington, where he cares for civilians in need.

POWERS: Doctor Mid-Nite is a brilliant physician and tactician who can see only in total darkness. He must wear special goggles of his own creation to see in daylight. Mid-Nite carries a variety of medications with him to help people in need. He also carries specially designed weapons called Blackout Bombs.

DOCTOR POLARIS

MAGNETIC MAYHEM

Doctor Neal Emerson suffers from a split personality disorder. As his normal self he is calm and rational (although strangely obsessed with magnets). But as Doctor Polaris he is terrifying! Polaris seeks to conquer the world—and he uses the power of magnetism to terrorize anyone that stands in his way.

Doctor Polaris used his magnetic powers to fashion his striking armor.

He can levitate by controlling the magnetic fields around him.

VITAL STATS

REAL NAME Doctor Neal Emerson

OCCUPATION Villain

HEIGHT 6ft 1in

WEIGHT 194 lbs

BASE Mobile

ALLIES Secret Society of Super-Villains

FOES The Flash

POWERS: Doctor Polaris can generate and control magnetic energy. He can attract, repel, or levitate anything made of metal. He can also absorb magnetic energy, although he must expel it quickly. Polaris doesn't possess any fighting skills, and his split personality makes him dangerously unstable.

POLARIS REBORN

Businessman and organized crime leader John Nichol studied the exploits of the original Doctor Polaris and took up the villain's mantle for a time. During his stint as the magnetic master, he battled the hero Blue Beetle and was part of an attack on the Justice Society.

DOCTOR PSYCHO
MIND MENACE

Doctor Psycho is a ruthless maniac who uses dreams and visions to manipulate people. Psycho has an intense hatred of women and sees Wonder Woman's defeat as his ultimate goal. He enjoys tormenting her friends in the hope that it will bring him one step closer to the Amazon princess herself.

VITAL STATS

REAL NAME Edgar Cizko
OCCUPATION Villain
HEIGHT 3ft 9in
WEIGHT 85 lbs
BASE Mobile
ALLIES Secret Society of Super-Villains
FOES Wonder Woman

Doctor Psycho uses trickery to mask his hideous face.

He is often mocked for his short stature.

MENTAL MASTER
Doctor Psycho lives to humiliate Wonder Woman. He attempts to destroy her self-worth by invading the dreams of her closest allies, turning them against her. He once used his mental abilities to make humanity lose faith in Wonder Woman and her Amazon friends.

POWERS: Doctor Psycho is able to create intense hallucinations inside the minds of his victims, leaving them in a nightmarish dream world. In these altered realities, Psycho preys on his victims' fears and often leaves them in a fragile state. He has below-average physical and possesses no fighting skills.

DOCTOR SIVANA
GENE GENIUS

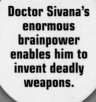

Doctor Sivana's enormous brainpower enables him to invent deadly weapons.

From his secret laboratory, the fiendish Doctor Sivana creates horribly mutated beasts and weapons of mass destruction in order to destroy the world. Sivana is a bitter man, angry at a society that constantly mocks him and foils his evil plans. He often dreams of the day that he finally defeats Captain Marvel.

VITAL STATS

REAL NAME Thaddeus Bodog Sivana

OCCUPATION Villain

HEIGHT 5ft 6in

WEIGHT 123 lbs

BASE Fawcett City

ALLIES Monster Society of Evil, Science Squad

FOES Captain Marvel

Sivana's feeble stature does not affect his genius mind.

CAUGHT BY MARVEL
Doctor Sivana formed a deadly alliance with Lex Luthor, hatching a complex scheme to dismantle Captain Marvel's life. After tracking Sivana down, a furious Marvel brought the mad scientist to justice!

POWERS: Doctor Sivana is a genius inventor. His specialty is combining animal and human genes to create mutated creatures. He often works with a group of evil scientists called the Science Squad, who share his passion for creating devices intended to destroy the world. Sivana possesses few, if any, fighting skills.

DONNA TROY
AMAZON WARRIOR

Donna Troy was raised and trained as a warrior on the planet New Cronus. She is the adopted sister of Wonder Woman, and, like her, she is a tireless warrior for justice. An original member of the Teen Titans, Donna is a loyal friend to her teammates and will defend their honor to the death.

VITAL STATS

REAL NAME Donna Troy
OCCUPATION Photographer, Hero
HEIGHT 5ft 9in
WEIGHT 140 lbs
BASE Mobile
ALLIES Teen Titans, Justice League of America
FOES Dark Angel

Donna looks so much like Wonder Woman that villains sometimes get the two mixed up.

She has served with the intergalactic police force called the Darkstars.

WONDER GIRL
Donna Troy is a mirror image of Wonder Woman. She was created by magic as a companion for Diana, but went on to forge her own heroic career as the first Wonder Girl. She was a founding member of the Teen Titans.

POWERS: Donna is a highly trained warrior, having studied with both the gods of New Cronus as well as the Amazons of Themyscira. She has super-strength, super-speed, and the power of flight. Donna can often coax unwilling people into telling the truth. She also shares a psychic link with Wonder Woman.

DOOM PATROL
HEROIC MISFITS

Doctor Niles Caulder took a gamble when he brought together various misfits of science in the hope that he could turn them into heroes. His gamble paid off. As the Doom Patrol, they've bravely risked their lives for mankind while struggling to make sense of a world that fears them.

MEMBERS INCLUDE

1 NEGATIVE MAN Larry Trainor can project a ghostly radioactive form from his body. Larry wraps himself in bandages so that his radioactivity does not harm others.

2 ROBOTMAN Cliff Steele's human brain is housed in a superpowered robot body. His own body was destroyed in an accident.

3 ELASTI-WOMAN Rita Farr can grow or shrink her body—or just one part of her body—to almost any size.

4 AMBUSH BUG Wacky Irwin Schwab found a bug-like alien suit which gave him the ability to teleport.

5 BUMBLEBEE Karen Beecher wears a special suit that enables her to shrink, fly, and fire electrical "stingers" at her enemies.

THE CHIEF
Niles Caulder (a.k.a. the Chief) has an amazing scientific mind, but is lacking in humanity. Although he claims to have brought the Doom Patrol together to help them as well as others, he often treats the team like lab rats. Caulder has been a wheelchair user since a life-saving operation left him paralyzed.

DOOMSDAY
THE DESTROYER

Doomsday is a monster from the planet Krypton, created by scientists to be a perfect, unstoppable killing machine. After being sent to Earth, Doomsday faced off against Superman in a monumental battle, nearly destroying Metropolis in the process. His current whereabouts are unknown.

VITAL STATS

REAL NAME None

OCCUPATION Villain

HEIGHT 7ft

WEIGHT 615 lbs

BASE Mobile

ALLIES Lex Luthor

FOES Superman

Doomsday's skin is covered in dangerous rocky spikes.

He has returned to Earth many times with varying degrees of intelligence.

DEATH OF SUPERMAN
The people of Metropolis will never forget the day that Superman died. After decimating the Justice League, Doomsday battled Superman in the middle of the city, eventually destroying the Man of Steel. Thankfully, Superman soon returned to life, but the event showed just what Doomsday is capable of, and he remains a serious threat.

POWERS: Doomsday's body has withstood the harshness of space for centuries. He is virtually indestructible and almost impossible to stop. Genetically programmed to seek combat, Doomsday will destroy anything in his path with a mindless rage. It is impossible to reason with him.

ECLIPSO
HEART OF DARKNESS

At one time, the Earth was covered by a thousand black diamond fragments.

When physicist Doctor Bruce Gordon was cut by a mystical black diamond, it unleashed Eclipso, an ancient spirit trapped for centuries. The spirit took control of Bruce and now, when darkness falls, he is transformed into the evil Eclipso.

VITAL STATS

REAL NAME Doctor Bruce Gordon
OCCUPATION Villain
HEIGHT 6ft 2in
WEIGHT 484 lbs
BASE Mobile
ALLIES Black Adam, Ian Karkull
FOES Spectre, Justice Society of America

As Eclipso is a spirit, he must attach himself to a human in order to do his evil work.

POWERS: The black diamond is also known as the Heart of Darkness. It gives Eclipso many powers, including super-strength and the ability to levitate. Eclipso also possesses invulnerability. He can shoot a powerful laser from his left eye, and a focused beam of black light from his right eye which paralyzes his foes.

BLACK DIAMOND
Eclipso has used the black diamond to take control of others besides Gordon. Jean Loring, the ex-wife of the Atom, found it in her cell at Arkham Asylum—Gotham's hospital for the criminally insane. Eclipso soon possessed her, using her insanity to fuel his evil powers.

ELONGATED MAN
STRETCHABLE SLEUTH

Whenever evil is afoot, wherever a mystery needs solving, that's where you'll find the Elongated Man. Although he now operates as a ghost detective, he remains an astute investigator with a great sense of humor. In life, he was a long-standing member of the Justice League, and has faced many foes.

VITAL STATS

REAL NAME Ralph Dibny

OCCUPATION Detective, Hero

HEIGHT 6ft 1in

WEIGHT 178 lbs

BASE Mobile

ALLIES Justice League of America, The Flash

FOES Felix Faust, Doctor Light

His nose twitches whenever a mystery is afoot.

Elongated Man was able to stretch all or just part of his body.

GHOST DETECTIVES
After Sue was murdered, Ralph threw himself into solving the mystery. Then he himself was struck down by the villain Felix Faust. Reunited in the afterlife, the happily married spirits investigate paranormal activity and continue their pursuit of adventure.

POWERS: Elongated Man is a brilliant detective and a trustworthy friend. When he was alive, he got his powers from an elixir called Gingold which is made from rare fruits. It allowed him to stretch his body to incredible lengths. As a ghost, Elongated Man can become invisible and possesses the power of flight.

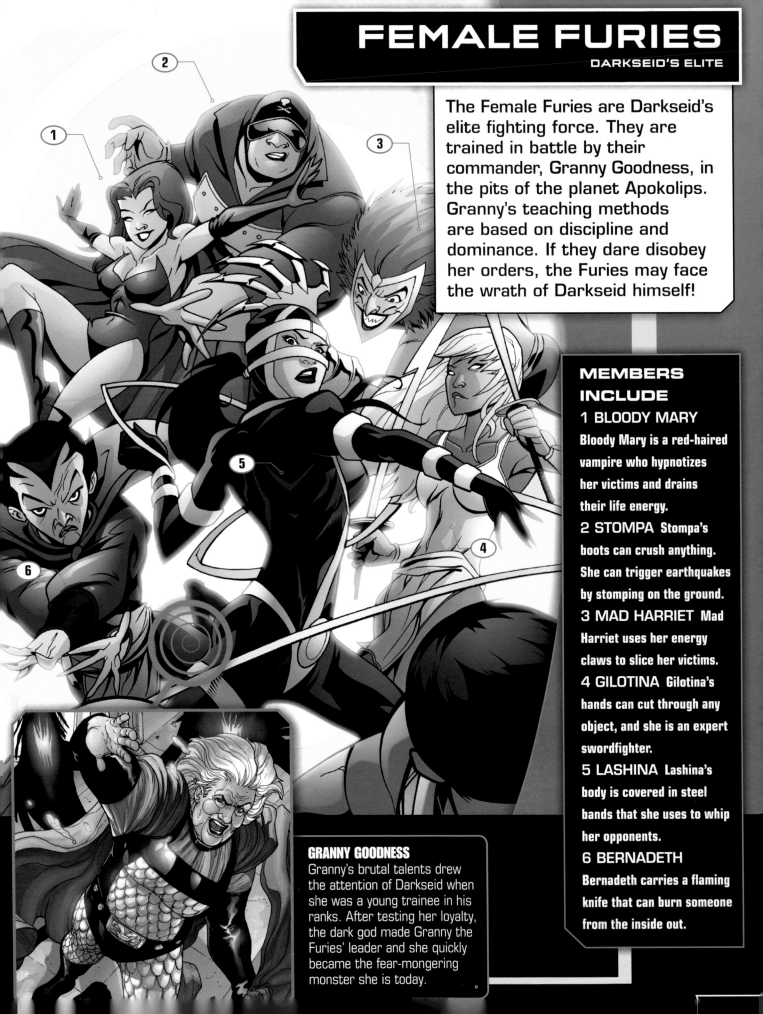

FEMALE FURIES
DARKSEID'S ELITE

The Female Furies are Darkseid's elite fighting force. They are trained in battle by their commander, Granny Goodness, in the pits of the planet Apokolips. Granny's teaching methods are based on discipline and dominance. If they dare disobey her orders, the Furies may face the wrath of Darkseid himself!

MEMBERS INCLUDE

1 BLOODY MARY Bloody Mary is a red-haired vampire who hypnotizes her victims and drains their life energy.

2 STOMPA Stompa's boots can crush anything. She can trigger earthquakes by stomping on the ground.

3 MAD HARRIET Mad Harriet uses her energy claws to slice her victims.

4 GILOTINA Gilotina's hands can cut through any object, and she is an expert swordfighter.

5 LASHINA Lashina's body is covered in steel bands that she uses to whip her opponents.

6 BERNADETH Bernadeth carries a flaming knife that can burn someone from the inside out.

GRANNY GOODNESS
Granny's brutal talents drew the attention of Darkseid when she was a young trainee in his ranks. After testing her loyalty, the dark god made Granny the Furies' leader and she quickly became the fear-mongering monster she is today.

FIRE
FLAMING STAR

Fire is a hot-headed Brazilian hero who's been a member of both the Justice League and the spy agency Checkmate. She is never afraid to speak her mind and enjoys debating with her teammates, although she usually knows when to cool it. When it comes to fighting for justice, Fire always brings the heat.

Originally Fire could only project flame from her mouth.

VITAL STATS

REAL NAME Beatriz Bonilla DaCosta

OCCUPATION Hero

HEIGHT 5ft 8in

WEIGHT 140 lbs

BASE Mobile

ALLIES Ice, Justice League of America

FOES Amanda Waller

She moonlights as a fashion model.

REUNITED

Evil businessman Maxwell Lord returned from the dead and set out to reunite past members of the Justice League—so he could destroy them! Together, Fire and her former teammates uncovered the mysteries behind Lord's resurrection.

POWERS: Fire was once exposed to a dangerous incendiary material. It gave her the ability to transform her body into a powerful green flame that she can manipulate and use to project energy blasts. She can also fly. Fire is an expert in many forms of combat and is a very skilled fighter and tactician.

FIRESTORM

THE NUCLEAR MAN

Ronnie controls Firestorm's body while Jason communicates with him telepathically.

When college jock Ronnie Raymond and teenager Jason Rusch concentrate, they fuse together into the hero known as Firestorm. At times, Ronnie and Jason have trouble getting along. Thankfully, they're aided by Professor Martin Stein, who helps them learn how to control their power—and their tempers!

VITAL STATS

REAL NAME Ronald "Ronnie" Raymond/Jason Rusch

OCCUPATION Hero

HEIGHT 6ft 1in (Raymond)/ 5ft 10in (Rusch)

WEIGHT 179 lbs (Raymond)/ 165 lbs (Rusch)

BASE Mobile

ALLIES Firehawk, The Atom

FOES Killer Frost, Black Bison

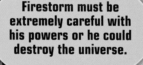

Firestorm must be extremely careful with his powers or he could destroy the universe.

FIRE ELEMENTAL

Professor Stein knows how hard life is for Ronnie and Jason because he was once Firestorm himself. As a fiery spirit called an elemental, he roamed space until driven mad by his own power. Stein was then freed from his elemental form and returned to Earth a normal man.

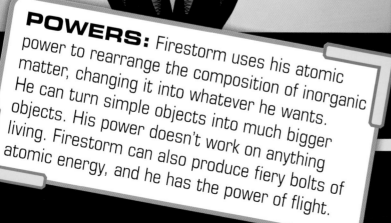

POWERS: Firestorm uses his atomic power to rearrange the composition of inorganic matter, changing it into whatever he wants. He can turn simple objects into much bigger objects. His power doesn't work on anything living. Firestorm can also produce fiery bolts of atomic energy, and he has the power of flight.

THE FLASH
SCARLET SPEEDSTER

When police scientist Barry Allen was doused with spilt chemicals, he became the Flash—the fastest man alive. Far from speedy himself, Barry has a hard time juggling the demands of his police job with his life as a hero. But while *Barry* may often show up late, the Flash is always right on time!

VITAL STATS

REAL NAME Bartholomew "Barry" Allen
OCCUPATION Police Scientist, Hero
HEIGHT 5ft 11in
WEIGHT 179 lbs
BASE Central City
ALLIES Green Lantern, Justice League of America
FOES The Rogues, Gorilla Grodd

The Flash's costume bears a lightning bolt symbol on the chest.

The Speed Force creates a protective electrical field around the Flash.

THE FLASH'S RING

As a busy scientist in the Central City Police Department, the Flash is always ready when evil strikes. He wears a spring-loaded ring which, when opened, releases his costume in an instant. The costume is made of pure energy created by the Speed Force.

POWERS: When Barry became the Flash, an extra-dimensional energy called the Speed Force was created. This allows the Flash to run at light speed and vibrate through solid objects, causing them to explode. The Flash can also lend his speed to other people. As Barry Allen, he's an expert scientist and criminologist.

FREEDOM FIGHTERS

LIBERTY AND JUSTICE FOR ALL

The Freedom Fighters have been battling evil since World War II, under the leadership of Uncle Sam. All the original members are long gone, but new heroes have taken on their names. Now under the watchful eye of a secret government agency, they continue the struggle to uphold justice.

MEMBERS INCLUDE

1 THE RAY Ray Terrill uses his light-based powers to blind his opponents.

2 HUMAN BOMB Andy Franklin creates explosions when his body contacts other objects. He wears a special suit to contain his powers.

3 FIREBRAND Andre Twist can manipulate fire. He's also a strong hand-to-hand combatant.

4 MISS AMERICA Joan Dale has the power to change the shape and size of any object.

5 UNCLE SAM Uncle Sam is the Spirit of America. He can grow to over 50 feet tall.

6 PHANTOM LADY Stormy Knight uses holographic wrist projectors to make herself invisible.

7 RED BEE Jenna Raleigh wears a suit of shiny red armor. She has recently mutated into a human and insect hybrid.

8 BLACK CONDOR John Trujillo can fly at great speeds and control the winds.

LET FREEDOM RING

Uncle Sam gets all his power from the strength of the American spirit. When that spirit falters, so does Sam's ability to grow into his giant form. Sam has seen his country through some dark times, but his belief in freedom never falters and he always remains optimistic about the future.

GANTHET
BLUE DEFENDER

Ganthet is one of the Guardians of the Universe, an ancient race that protects the universe from evil. They are the creators of the Green Lantern Corps police force. Unlike most Guardians, who do not even take names, Ganthet stands proudly as an individual. He now serves as a Green Lantern himself.

VITAL STATS

REAL NAME Ganthet
OCCUPATION Guardian of the Universe
HEIGHT 3ft 2in
WEIGHT 65 lbs
BASE Oa
ALLIES Green Lantern
FOES Larfleeze, Sinestro

Ganthet wears a ponytail as symbol of his individuality.

Like all Guardians, he has blue skin.

THE PLANET OA
The Guardians of the Universe reside on the celestial planet of Oa. The planet is known for its intricate architecture, and also houses the Central Battery of the Green Lantern Corps. Though they keep an eye on the entire universe, the Guardians rarely leave the safety of Oa.

POWERS: Ganthet is immortal. He also possesses the powers of telepathy, telekinesis, and flight. As a Guardian, he has access to the Central Power Battery, where huge amounts of cosmic energy are stored. As a Green Lantern, Ganthet uses his ring to create hard-light energy constructs (solid objects made of light).

GENERAL ZOD
KRYPTONIAN CRIMINAL

No one locks up General Zod and gets away with it! The cruel Kryptonian criminal was jailed by Superman's father, Jor-El, inside the ghostly world known as the Phantom Zone. Now Zod blames Superman for his lengthy imprisonment and vows that one day he will make the Man of Steel kneel before him.

Zod's uniform indicates that he is a Kryptonian criminal.

VITAL STATS
REAL NAME Dru-Zod
OCCUPATION Villain
HEIGHT 6ft 3in
WEIGHT 195 lbs
BASE The Phantom Zone
ALLIES Ursa, Non
FOES Superman

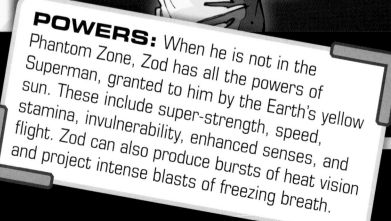

PHANTOM ZONE CRIMINALS
Zod and his accomplices Ursa and Non were found guilty of crimes against Krypton, and banished by Superman's father to the desolate and ethereal Phantom Zone. It was in the Phantom Zone that Zod's hatred for the El family grew stronger each day.

POWERS: When he is not in the Phantom Zone, Zod has all the powers of Superman, granted to him by the Earth's yellow sun. These include super-strength, speed, stamina, invulnerability, enhanced senses, and flight. Zod can also produce bursts of heat vision and project intense blasts of freezing breath.

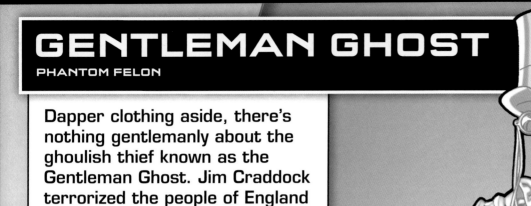

GENTLEMAN GHOST
PHANTOM FELON

Dapper clothing aside, there's nothing gentlemanly about the ghoulish thief known as the Gentleman Ghost. Jim Craddock terrorized the people of England in the late 1800s, until he was caught and put to death. After mysteriously rising from the grave, he continues his life of crime in a ghostly spirit form.

Gentleman Ghost usually makes his face invisible because it is horribly decayed.

He uses an antique flintlock pistol to stop his enemies in their tracks.

VITAL STATS
REAL NAME James "Jim" Craddock
OCCUPATION Criminal
HEIGHT 5ft 11in
WEIGHT Inapplicable
BASE Mobile
ALLIES Injustice Society
FOES Hawkman, Justice Society

Gentleman Ghost's cane shoots phantom fire from its tip.

INJUSTICE MEMBER
Gentleman Ghost often teams up with the Injustice Society, whose members include Icicle, Tigress, Wizard, and Solomon Grundy. The evil allies recently tried to kidnap Stargirl, resulting in an enormous battle with the Justice Society.

POWERS: The Gentleman Ghost is a specter who can become invisible and pass through solid objects. His ghostly form renders him immortal, and recently he has developed the power to summon vengeful spirits from his enemies' pasts. The Gentlemen Ghost is an average fighter and an excellent marksman.

GEO-FORCE
EARTH-SHAKER

Geo-Force is the superpowered prince of the European country of Markovia. Beneath his quiet, aloof exterior lies the mind of a true hero. As the leader of the Outsiders super hero team, Geo-Force takes his role very seriously. After all, a hero with powers over the whole Earth needs to stay grounded.

Geo-Force cannot stay away from Earth for too long, otherwise his powers will fade.

His belt helps him to control his powers.

VITAL STATS
REAL NAME Brion Markov
OCCUPATION Prince, Hero
HEIGHT 6ft 4in
WEIGHT 220 lbs
BASE Markovia
ALLIES Batman, The Outsiders
FOES Deathstroke

POWERS: Geo-Force has control over the Earth itself. He is able to alter gravity with a wave of his hand, and can also manipulate solid rock and project lava blasts. Geo-Force possesses super-strength and endurance. Recently, his abilities were enhanced, however his true power levels remain untested.

PRINCE OF MARKOVIA
Geo-Force is a proud king as well as a formidable opponent on the battlefield. He has often used his powers in the defense of his country, Markovia, and his loyal subjects are grateful for his protection. Although he puts his own people first, Geo-Force is a friend to all with good intentions and sometimes grants asylum to heroes who are in need.

GIGANTA

BIG AND BAD

Frail Doctor Doris Zuel hoped to transfer her brilliant mind into the body of Wonder Woman. But after a failed experiment, Doris's mind ended up in the body of a shape-changing circus performer. Now, as the monstrous, super-sized Giganta, Doris blames the amazing Amazon for her horrible condition.

VITAL STATS

REAL NAME Doctor Doris Zuel
OCCUPATION Villain
HEIGHT 6ft 6in
WEIGHT 246 lbs
BASE Ivy Town
ALLIES Villainy Inc.
FOES Wonder Woman

Giganta's intellect decreases as she grows in size.

Giganta's suit is designed to expand as her size increases.

VILLAINY INC.

Giganta's body is that of a former circus strong woman named Olga. Even in her new form, Giganta was unable to defeat Wonder Woman alone so she banded together with the evil Queen Clea, Cyborgirl, and Doctor Poison in a team known as Villainy Inc.

POWERS: Originally, Giganta could grow from her regular human size to 50 feet tall in seconds. Over the years, her powers have evolved and she can now grow hundreds of feet. When Giganta grows she gains super-strength, though her giant body can be difficult to manage. She is also an accomplished scientist.

GORILLA GRODD
CONQUEROR APE

Gorilla Grodd is a super-intelligent ape who developed extraordinary mental powers after a spaceship crashed near his jungle home in Africa. Grodd uses his gifts to enslave the human race, and has hatched many bloodthirsty plans to take over the world. Thankfully, the Flash has upset them all.

Grodd often wears a device that amplifies his mental powers, but can manage without it.

Although he hates most humans he is a member of the Secret Society of Super-Villains.

VITAL STATS

REAL NAME Grodd
OCCUPATION Villain
HEIGHT 6ft 6in
WEIGHT 600 lbs
BASE Gorilla City
ALLIES Secret Society of Super-Villains
FOES The Flash

POWERS: Gorilla Grodd is a master of mind control and can transfer his own brilliant mind into someone else's body. His powers are so strong that he can mentally project intense beams of energy at a chosen target. Although Grodd is a scientific genius and inventor, he still retains his ferocious animal nature.

GORILLA WARFARE
Grodd and his angry apes once declared war on humanity. They traveled from their home in Gorilla City to America and attacked the Justice League, turning the heroes into apes themselves. Eventually peace was restored and the "JLApe" returned to normal.

GREEN ARROW

EMERALD ARCHER

Millionaire playboy Oliver Queen had it all—until the day his boat crashed on a desert island, leaving him stranded. In order to survive, Oliver had to hunt. He used objects he found in the jungle to make a bow, and taught himself archery. Now back on U.S. soil, Oliver uses his skills as the hotshot hero Green Arrow.

VITAL STATS

REAL NAME Oliver Jonas Queen
OCCUPATION Adventurer, Hero
HEIGHT 5ft 11in
WEIGHT 185 lbs
BASE Mobile
ALLIES Black Canary, Green Lantern
FOES Merlyn, Shado

Green Arrow has trick arrows in his quiver for almost every occasion.

Green Arrow protects a mysterious forest in the middle of Star City.

WEDDING NIGHTMARE

Green Arrow and Black Canary planned a peaceful wedding, but things didn't quite go to plan. First their nuptials were interrupted by an attack from the Injustice League. Then, during their honeymoon, the groom was revealed to be a villain called Everyman in disguise.

POWERS: Green Arrow is a world-class archer and uses a variety of archery equipment. His special weapons include explosive arrows, smoke arrows, and knockout arrows. He has also been known to use the occasional boxing glove arrow. Green Arrow is a superior hand-to-hand combatant and street fighter.

GREEN LANTERN
EMERALD KNIGHT

Green Lantern's ring must be recharged every 24 hours.

Cocky test pilot Hal Jordan never played by the rules. Then a dying alien gave him a special ring—and a new sense of duty. Hal became Earth's Green Lantern, a member of the interstellar police force. He's now committed to protecting the universe, though he often clashes with his Guardian bosses.

Green Lantern's costume is generated by his ring.

VITAL STATS
REAL NAME Hal Jordan
OCCUPATION Pilot, Hero
HEIGHT 6ft 2in
WEIGHT 186 lbs
BASE Coast City
ALLIES Green Arrow, The Flash
FOES Sinestro, Hector Hammond

ABIN SUR
Hal Jordan was given his Green Lantern ring by Corps member Abin Sur, who had crash-landed his spaceship on Earth while investigating a prophecy about the end of the universe. As Abin was one of the most respected members of the Corps, Hal knew he had big shoes to fill.

POWERS: Hal's Green Lantern ring can create hard-light energy constructs (solid forms made of light) in any shape he can imagine. The ring is also useful for space travel as it can double as a map and universal translator, but it must be recharged using a lantern-shaped battery. Hal is also a skilled athlete and fighter.

THE GREEN LANTERN CORPS
PROTECTORS OF THE GALAXY

The Green Lantern Corps is an interstellar police force that protects all 3,600 sectors of the galaxy. It was created billions of years ago by tiny blue-skinned aliens called the Guardians of the Universe. New recruits to the Corps are trained on the planet Oa, where they learn to use and control the emerald energy of their power rings. This force comes from an entity called Ion, whose willpower fuels each ring.

MANHUNTERS
Before they created the Green Lantern Corps, the Guardians of the Universe had tried other ways of keeping peace in the galaxy. They once built a fleet of heartless robots called the Manhunters, who patrolled the cosmos as a mechanical police force. The Manhunters eventually rebelled and the Guardians had to catch and destroy as many as they could.

MEMBERS INCLUDE

Hal Jordan, Guy Gardner, John Stewart, Kyle Rayner, Kilowog, Sodam Yat, Arisia, Salaak, Soranik Natu, Stel, Tomar Tu, Chaselon, Mogo, Abin Sur, Isamot

GUY GARDNER
EMERALD WARRIOR

Guy always says exactly what is on his mind, whether others want to hear it or not.

Guy Gardner is one of Earth's Green Lanterns. He can sometimes be difficult to deal with and enjoys challenging the Guardians' leadership, much to their displeasure. Though a bit outspoken, Guy is also honest and direct—something that has earned him the respect of his Green Lantern colleagues.

VITAL STATS
REAL NAME Guy Gardner
OCCUPATION Hero, Green Lantern
HEIGHT 6ft
WEIGHT 180 lbs
BASE Oa
ALLIES John Stewart, Kilowog
FOES Sinestro

Guy's impulsive behavior makes his energy constructs volatile.

He runs a bar known as Warriors especially for Green Lanterns.

POWERS: Using his Green Lantern ring, Guy can generate hard-light energy constructs (solid objects made from light) by forming an image of them in his mind. The ring can also be used as a map and translator when traveling in space. Guy is a skilled fighter, although his t... gift is saying the wrong thi...

GUY GARDNER—WARRIOR
For a brief time, Guy Gardner had the power to morph his body into any weapon he chose. It was the result of experimentation by an alien race known as the Vuldarians. Eventually Guy's body rejected the changes and he returned to being a normal Green Lantern.

HARLEY QUINN
THE JOKER'S GIRLFRIEND

Harley Quinn was once the Joker's therapist—now she's his devoted girlfriend! She helps the grinning madman plan his most diabolical schemes. The Joker often dismisses her affections, but Harley continues to adore her "Mister J." Recently, she has found friendship with fellow villains Poison Ivy and Catwoman.

VITAL STATS

REAL NAME Doctor Harleen Quinzel
OCCUPATION Criminal
HEIGHT 5ft 7in
WEIGHT 140 lbs
BASE Gotham City
ALLIES The Joker, Poison Ivy
FOES Batman, Robin

Harley uses a pop-gun to disorient her enemies.

Her costume resembles a jester's colorful suit.

MAD LOVE

Harley Quinn was a respected doctor, helping to rehabilitate Gotham City's worst criminals. She never imagined that she would fall for one of them! However, after spending time with the Joker, she became drawn into his insane world and decided to join him in his life of crime.

POWERS: Harley is a gifted acrobat whose abilities have been enhanced by one of Poison Ivy's herbal remedies. She is an average fighter whose bag of tricks contains a variety of joke-themed weapons, such as a pop-gun and oversized mallet. Though Harley was a therapist, she has become dangerously unbalanced.

HAWK AND DOVE
A FORCE OF BALANCE

Like their bird namesakes, Hawk and Dove are total opposites: Hank has a violent temper while Dawn is peaceful and calm. The duo represent the balance of order and chaos in the universe. They are often at odds with one another, but their differences help them to keep each other in check while fighting crime.

They were given their powers by the mystical Lords of Order and Chaos.

VITAL STATS

HAWK
REAL NAME Hank Hall
OCCUPATION Hero
HEIGHT 5ft 10in
WEIGHT 181 lbs
BASE Mobile
ALLIES Dove, Birds of Prey
FOES Kestrel

DOVE
REAL NAME Dawn Granger
OCCUPATION Hero
HEIGHT 5ft 6in
WEIGHT 125 lbs
BASE Mobile
ALLIES Hawk, Birds of Prey
FOES Kestrel

POWERS:
When danger is near Hank and Dawn need only call out their names—"Hawk!" and "Dove!"—to trigger their transformation. When in their Hawk and Dove forms they both possess super strength, endurance, and speed.

ORIGINAL DUO
The original Dove was Hawk's younger brother, Don Hall. Don's calm demeanor and level head often helped to temper Hank's impulsive outbursts. Tragically, Don perished while heroically protecting a young child from a deadly shadow-demon.

HAWKGIRL
BIRD OF ETERNITY

Hawkgirl has lived many lives. She was born in ancient Egypt, but a villainous priest named Hath-Set cursed her to be reborn through the ages, never finding true peace. Hawkgirl's lives are spent battling injustice and she has faced many dangers, but her love for Hawkman always brings her safely home.

VITAL STATS

REAL NAME Shiera Hall
OCCUPATION Hero
HEIGHT 5ft 7in
WEIGHT 123 lbs
BASE St. Roch
ALLIES Hawkman, Justice League of America
FOES Shadow Thief, Gentleman Ghost

Hawkgirl's Nth metal belt gives her the power of flight.

A spear is Hawkgirl's favorite weapon when she is battling evil.

QUEEN OF HAWKWORLD

Hawkgirl's mother is the evil Queen Khea. She rules over Hawkworld, a dimension populated by dangerous half-man, half-animal beasts. Together with the priest Hath-Set, Khea plotted to destroy Hawkgirl and Hawkman and trap them in Hawkworld forever.

POWERS: Hawkgirl has super-strength, speed, and endurance thanks to the Nth metal belt she wears. This metal is a precious resource from the planet Thanagar that has mysterious and powerful properties. Nth metal also enables Hawkgirl to fly and gives her the ability to heal quickly from injury.

HAWKMAN
WINGED WARRIOR

Hawkman's harness is made with Nth Metal, and enables him to fly.

Hawkman is a warrior prince who has been reborn dozens of times through the centuries. Currently he is archaeologist Carter Hall, a curator at the Stonechat Museum. In each life Hawkman is fated to meet and fall in love with his wife, Hawkgirl. Using weapons from the past, he battles evil alongside her.

VITAL STATS
REAL NAME Carter Hall
OCCUPATION Hero
HEIGHT 6ft 1in
WEIGHT 195 lbs
BASE St. Roch
ALLIES Hawkgirl, The Atom
FOES Shadow Thief, Gentleman Ghost

Hawkman uses a heavy, spiked mace during battle.

POWERS: Hawkman wears a golden harness made of Nth metal, which gives him many powers. These include super-strength, speed, endurance, flight, and self-healing. He uses a variety of ancient weapons in battle, including a shield, a mace, and, on occasion, a mystical battle glove called the Claw of Horus.

PRINCE KHUFU
In his first life, Hawkman was a noble Prince named Khufu. As Egyptian head-of-state, he proudly ruled the sands of Egypt alongside his wife, Chay-Ara. The couple lived a life of bliss, until the envious Hath-Set sought to destroy their love forever.

HECTOR HAMMOND

MENTAL MONSTER

Contact with an alien meteorite gave scientist Hector Hammond telepathic powers, but swelled his head to gigantic proportions. Hammond somehow blamed Green Lantern, and swore his revenge. Now he plays a dangerous game of cat and mouse with the hero, though his master plan is as yet unknown.

Hammond is no longer able to speak and must communicate telepathically.

VITAL STATS

REAL NAME Hector Hammond
OCCUPATION Villain
HEIGHT 5ft 1in
WEIGHT 156 lbs
BASE Mobile
ALLIES Ophidian
FOES Green Lantern

He must remain strapped to a special chair, otherwise he cannot stay upright.

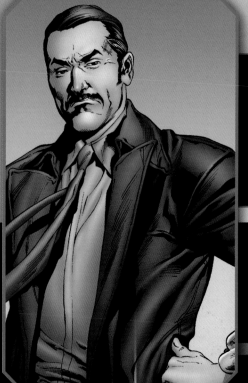

JEALOUS GUY

While working for Ferris Aircraft, the jealous Hammond did his best to destroy a budding romance between company president Carol Ferris and Hal Jordan. Later, with his mind and body horribly transformed, his hatred for Jordan grew even stronger.

POWERS: In his mutated state, Hector Hammond has a genius-level intellect and the ability to read a person's most private thoughts. He has also exhibited strong telepathic and telekinetic powers when focused. His body, however, is paralyzed, requiring him to sit motionless in his specially designed chair.

HIPPOLYTA
AMAZON QUEEN

She is thousands of years old but has the appearance of a young woman.

The stately Hippolyta is Queen of the Amazons and the mother of Wonder Woman. Her home is the tropical island of Themyscira. Though she rules peacefully and is kind to those of goodwill, woe betide anyone who threatens her people! Hippolyta is a warrior at heart and will defend her Amazon sisters to the death.

Hippolyta wears a traditional Amazon suit of armor.

VITAL STATS
REAL NAME Hippolyta
OCCUPATION Queen
HEIGHT 5ft 9in
WEIGHT 150 lbs
BASE Themyscira
ALLIES Wonder Woman, Donna Troy
FOES Ares, Circe

POWERS: The gods of Olympus granted Hippolyta immortality, along with incredible strength, speed, and agility. She was also given the Golden Girdle of Gaea, a belt that magically protects Hippolyta and her fellow Amazons. She is trained in a variety of fighting styles and wears ceremonial armor in battle.

AMAZONS ATTACK
The noble Hippolyta is fiercely protective of Wonder Woman. She once launched an assault on Washington, D.C. when she believed her daughter was wrongfully accused of a crime. It was later revealed that the villainous sorceress Circe manipulated Hippolyta and the Amazons into attacking.

HOURMAN
HERO OF THE HOUR

Rick Taylor followed in his father's footsteps to become Hourman—a hero whose time is always now. Rick's powers only last for an hour at a time, but he packs a lot of action into that hour. He's a member of the legendary Justice Society of America and is married to his teammate, Liberty Belle.

His special hourglass allows him to see visions of the future.

Miraclo makes Hourman's body resistant to harm

VITAL STATS
REAL NAME Rick Tyler
OCCUPATION Artist, Hero
HEIGHT 5ft 9in
WEIGHT 170 lbs
BASE New York City
ALLIES Liberty Belle, Justice Society of America
FOES Wizard, Icicle

HOURMAN OF THE FUTURE
An android version of Hourman, created by Rick Tyler's father, protected the 853rd century. He possessed all the accumulated knowledge of his human predecessors. This Hourman was also a member of the JSA.

POWERS: Hourman has enhanced strength, speed, and agility thanks to a substance called Miraclo which he absorbs into his body through his wrist gauntlets. He also has visions, or "flash forwards," where he can see events one hour into the future—though in many cases he's powerless to stop them.

HUNTRESS
NIGHT STALKER

Helena Bertinelli was raised in a family of criminals. After seeing the misery caused by their evil ways, she dedicated her life to protecting innocents as the Huntress. Though her brutal tactics sometimes get her into trouble with Batman, Huntress is a committed member of the heroic Birds of Prey team.

The Huntress can speak fluent Italian.

Her costume is dark in color so she can blend into the night.

VITAL STATS
REAL NAME Helena Bertinelli
OCCUPATION Hero
HEIGHT 5ft 11in
WEIGHT 148 lbs
BASE Gotham City
ALLIES Birds of Prey, The Question
FOES Lady Shiva, Man-Bat

STRAINED RELATIONSHIP
When the Huntress first appeared in Gotham City, Batman was hesitant to accept her because of her harsh methods of justice. He monitored her behavior for a trial period, and after seeing positive changes he welcomed Huntress into his circle of trust.

POWERS: Huntress is an agile gymnast and acrobat. She's also trained in many different fighting styles. Her favorite mode of transport is a customized motorcycle, and her weapon of choice is a miniature crossbow. Huntress can be stubborn, but she is slowly learning to work well with other heroes.

HUSH
A FRIEND FOR NEVER

Hush is a cold-blooded villain bent on destroying Batman's life. But it was not always that way. As children, Tommy Elliot and Bruce Wayne were best friends, until a terrible accident drove them apart. As an adult, Hush blames the Dark Knight for his misfortune and the two are now bitter enemies.

Hush covers himself with bandages to conceal his identity.

VITAL STATS
REAL NAME Doctor Thomas "Tommy" Elliot
OCCUPATION Villain
HEIGHT 6ft 1in
WEIGHT 200 lbs
BASE Gotham City
ALLIES The Riddler
FOES Batman, Catwoman

Guns are his favorite weapons.

CHILDHOOD FRIENDS
Tommy Elliot reappeared in Bruce Wayne's life after many years. He seemed to be a friend—but after learning of Bruce's secret life as Batman, Elliot began plotting to destroy him. After adopting the Hush identity, Elliot employed Gotham City's worst criminals to take down the Dark Knight.

POWERS: Hush's obsession with beating Batman drove him to become the best at everything. He used his great wealth to pay for training in many different skills, and is now a world-class fighter and expert marksman. He also has a brilliant tactical mind. Hush's alter-ego, Doctor Tommy Elliot, is an exceptional surgeon.

ICE
FROSTY FRIEND

Her hair is as white as snow.

Shy Tora Olafsdotter wanted to use her powers to help people. She ran away from her manipulative grandfather to join the Justice League as the hero Ice, where she found an unlikely best friend in her outgoing teammate Fire. Ice may have a cold touch, but everyone agrees that she also has a warm heart.

VITAL STATS

REAL NAME Tora Olafsdotter
OCCUPATION Hero
HEIGHT 5ft 7in
WEIGHT 136 lbs
BASE Mobile
ALLIES Fire, Guy Gardner
FOES Overmaster

Ice prefers the comfort of the Arctic winds to warm locations.

CHILLING CHILDHOOD
When Ice was a little girl, her father taught her to keep her powers a secret in case her grandfather tried to use them for evil. Ice felt hurt and confused, and she dealt with it by locking away the memories of her childhood. Only recently has she unleashed her full potential.

POWERS: Ice can generate intense bursts of cold from her fingers, creating sharp ice shards to use as weapons. Her powers can be used in a restrained way, but recently they have grown wild and uncontrollable. Now, when Ice powers up, her skin turns blue and she's capable of creating blizzard-like weather.

IMPULSE
QUICK KID

Young Irey West inherited her super speedster powers from her father Wally West, the former Flash. As Impulse, she uses her speed to help those in need. Although she's a hero, Impulse is still a little girl, so her parents keep a close eye on her to ensure she doesn't get into *too* much trouble.

VITAL STATS
REAL NAME Iris "Irey" West
OCCUPATION Elementary School Student, Hero
HEIGHT 4ft 2in
WEIGHT 50 lbs
BASE Keystone City
ALLIES The Flash, Kid Flash
FOES Queen Bee, Gorilla Grodd

Impulse loves wearing her lightning-shaped hair clips.

Her costume is made from Speed Force energy.

JAI WEST
Impulse has a twin brother, Jai West. Jai was also born with super-speed, and both children were set to become heroes. That changed when the villain Zoom corrupted the Speed Force, making it fatal for both twins to connect to it. Impulse was forced to absorb her brother's power in order to save his life.

POWERS: Impulse can run at super-speed and has the ability to vibrate her body so she can pass through solid objects. She's also surrounded by a protective aura when traveling at high speeds. Impulse is filled with excitement and youthful enthusiasm. She is anxious to learn how to be a hero, like her dad.

Sodam Yat, of the planet Daxam, is the current host of the Ion entity.

Ion has existed since the Earth was created. His willpower fuels the entire Green Lantern Corps. For centuries, the Guardians of the Universe kept him a secret, fearing that evil forces would corrupt him. Now Ion's positive spirit is free—and ready to choose the next Green Lantern who will wield his power.

Ion's power does not require a ring to create constructs.

VITAL STATS
REAL NAME Ion
OCCUPATION Willpower Entity
HEIGHT Undetermined
WEIGHT Undetermined
BASE Mobile
ALLIES Green Lantern, Guardians of the Universe
FOES Sinestro

TORCHBEARER
Ion's energy was first bestowed upon Kyle Rayner by the Guardians, who believed him to be the Torchbearer of prophecy who would lead the Green Lantern Corps. However, they eventually decided that Sodam Yat was better suited to wield Ion's power.

POWERS: Ion is the immortal embodiment of willpower, and seeks exceptional Green Lantern Torchbearers on whom to bestow his power. When in possession of Ion's energy, a Green Lantern's abilities become unlimited. Ion amplifies their will, enabling them to manipulate time and space.

ISIS
HUMAN GODDESS

Slave Adrianna Tomaz fell in love with her master, the powerful Black Adam. As a gift, he shared his power with her. Now, as the mighty Isis, she hopes to warm her husband's cold heart. Isis sees the good in everything around her and encourages Black Adam to do the same and join her on a quest for justice.

Adrianna is transformed by shouting "I am Isis!"

VITAL STATS
REAL NAME Adrianna Tomaz
OCCUPATION Hero
HEIGHT 5ft 10in
WEIGHT 139 lbs
BASE Kahndaq
ALLIES Black Adam
FOES Felix Faust

Her powers are stored in her Amulet of Isis, a gift from Black Adam.

BLACK ADAM
Isis fell in love with Black Adam after he freed her from a life of servitude, and she hopes to inspire him to be a kinder and gentler ruler. They have faced many struggles together, and have even found the strength to overcome death itself.

POWERS: Isis has the ability to heal things, including plant, animal, and, in some cases, human life. She can also soothe tensions and bring out the positive attributes in those around her. As a member of the Black Marvel family she also has super-strength, the power of flight, and resistance to injury.

JADE
PROTECTOR OF THE STARHEART

The symbol on her costume represents the Starheart.

Jade is the daughter of Alan Scott, the original Green Lantern, and proudly carries on her family's legacy. She has seen her fair share of triumph and tragedy over the years, but continues to serve as a hero, protecting the cosmic power source known as the Starheart alongside her twin, Obsidian.

VITAL STATS
REAL NAME Jennifer-Lynn Hayden
OCCUPATION Protector of the Starheart, Hero
HEIGHT 5ft 5in
WEIGHT 123 lbs
BASE Mobile
ALLIES Green Lantern
FOES Eclipso

Jade has star-shaped birthmarks on the palms of her hands.

LANTERN'S LOVE
Jade became close to Green Lantern Kyle Rayner, and their friendship evolved into a romantic relationship. The pair went through many ups and downs, and soon realized that their schedules as heroes made it difficult for them find time for each other.

POWERS: Jade's body can harness the force of the Starheart, a green crystal. Using its power, she is able to create green energy constructs similar to those of a Green Lantern. The Starheart power also gives Jade the ability to fly. Jade and her twin brother Obsidian are connected by a low-level psychic link.

JAKEEM THUNDER
PROTECTOR OF THE THUNDERBOLT

Jakeem Thunder was a teenage troublemaker. Then one day he was given a pen that released the Thunderbolt, a magical genie from the 5th Dimension. At first Jakeem used the genie's powers selfishly, but after joining the Justice Society he learned a whole new set of values. Now he works hard at being a hero.

VITAL STATS

REAL NAME Jakeem John Williams

OCCUPATION High School Student, Hero

HEIGHT 5ft 4in

WEIGHT 140 lbs

BASE Keystone City

ALLIES Justice Society of America

FOES Ultra-Humanite

The Thunderbolt is made up of magical pink lightning.

JOHNNY THUNDER

The Thunderbolt's first master was Johnny Thunder, a kind-hearted young man who served with the Justice Society during World War II. Johnny was not very smart, so the Thunderbolt often helped him out when he had got himself into a jam.

POWERS: When Jakeem says the words "so cool," the magical Thunderbolt genie is released from his pen. The genie can grant Jakeem anything he desires, from a new skateboard to victory in battle. It can't, however, protect him all the time, so he's taken up fight training with his Justice Society teammates.

JIM GORDON
COMMITTED COMMISSIONER

Gotham City Police Commissioner James Gordon has been a trusted friend to Batman since both men began their crime-fighting careers. Jim is a respected member of the force, and knows he can rely on his fellow officers—and Batman—to help protect the city they all love so much.

Gordon activates the Bat-Signal to summon Batman.

VITAL STATS
REAL NAME James W. Gordon
OCCUPATION Gotham City Police Commissioner
HEIGHT 5ft 9in
WEIGHT 168 lbs
BASE Gotham City
ALLIES Batman, Robin
FOES The Joker, Two-Face

FRIEND OF THE BAT
Although he was initially wary of Batman, Commissioner Gordon grew to respect him. He sees the difference the Dark Knight makes to the people of Gotham City. Gordon often defends Batman to his colleagues in the police department, who are sometimes sceptical.

POWERS: Jim Gordon is one of the most dedicated members of the Gotham City Police Department. He is a highly skilled detective and an expert criminologist. Jim's police training has also made him an above-average hand-to-hand fighter, and he's known for his fierce left hook. He also carries a gun to protect himself.

JIMMY OLSEN
SUPERMAN'S PAL

Jimmy Olsen is a photographer for the *Daily Planet* and one of the most famous people in Metropolis. There isn't anywhere Jimmy won't go to get a good photo, and he often ends up putting himself in the line of fire. Thankfully, Jimmy is best friends with Superman, who is always there to bail him out.

Jimmy Olsen is never without his trusty camera and press pass.

VITAL STATS

REAL NAME James Bartholomew Olsen

OCCUPATION Photographer, Journalist

HEIGHT 5ft 9in

WEIGHT 165 lbs

BASE Metropolis

ALLIES Superman, Lois Lane

FOES Darkseid

SUPER JIMMY

Jimmy is a magnet for trouble and adventure. After an encounter with an alien virus, Jimmy was temporarily transformed into a stretchy super hero known as Elastic-Lad. On a number of occasions, he has also turned into Turtle Boy.

POWERS: Jimmy Olsen has no special powers and he is an average athlete and fighter. However, Jimmy has experienced a variety of mutations over the years, through accidents, experiments, and otherworldly encounters, which have given him incredible abilities for short periods of time.

JOHN STEWART

GREEN GUARDIAN

When Hal Jordan was injured in battle, former U.S. Marine John Stewart proudly replaced him as Earth's Green Lantern. Like Kyle Rayner and Guy Gardner, he's a member of the Lantern Honor Guard—an elite few Green Lanterns who operate in all sectors of the galaxy.

Like his fellow Lantern, Guy Gardner, John Stewart does not wear a mask.

VITAL STATS

REAL NAME John Stewart
OCCUPATION Architect, Green Lantern
HEIGHT 6ft 1in
WEIGHT 200 lbs
BASE Earth, Oa
ALLIES Hal Jordan, Guy Gardner
FOES Fatality

DARKSTARS

When the Green Lantern Corps disbanded for a while, John Stewart was drafted by an intergalactic peacekeeping force called the Darkstars. The Darkstars would later be torn apart by Grayven, a villain who claimed to be the tyrant Darkseid's son

POWERS: John's power ring can generate hard-light energy constructs (solid objects made of light) in any shape he imagines. It also acts as a map and universal translator— useful when traveling in space. John's military training has put him in peak physical condition and he is a skilled athlete and...

THE JOKER
CLOWN PRINCE OF CRIME

The Joker is a crazy criminal mastermind with a horrific, clown-like appearance. But there's nothing funny about the Joker's cruel and dangerous pranks. He blames Batman for his ghoulish look and vows to destroy the Dark Knight.

VITAL STATS

REAL NAME Unknown

OCCUPATION Villain

HEIGHT 6ft 5in

WEIGHT 192 lbs

BASE Gotham City

ALLIES Harley Quinn

FOES Batman

The Joker has been known to use a deck of playing cards as a weapon.

The Joker's flower shoots a deadly chemical acid.

THE RED HOOD
The Joker was once a small-time criminal known as the Red Hood. While being chased by Batman, the Red Hood slipped and fell into a vat of chemical acid. He emerged horribly changed, with stark white skin, green hair, a ghoulish grin, a crazy laugh—and a desire to get even with Batman!

POWERS: The Joker's favorite weapon is his poisonous Joker Venom, which leaves his victims with a ghastly smile frozen on their faces. Over time, the Joker has built up immunity to his own venom and is resistant to pain. He is an average fighter, but likes to use a range of weapons, including a deadly flower.

JONAH HEX
MAD MARKSMAN

Apaches scarred Hex's face with the Mark of the Demon after he broke a sacred law.

Jonah Hex is a famous gunslinger from the Wild West. He's first and foremost a bounty hunter, but he has also made a vow to protect the innocent. Jonah has a bad reputation, a fearsome appearance, and a gruff attitude. But make no mistake—Jonah Hex will do whatever it takes to bring villains to justice.

VITAL STATS
REAL NAME Jonah Woodson Hex
OCCUPATION Bounty Hunter
HEIGHT 5ft 11in
WEIGHT 189 lbs
BASE Late 19th century
ALLIES Joshua Dazzleby
FOES Quentin Turnbull

He carries a Colt pistol to defend himself.

POWERS: Jonah is an exceptional marksman. He's quick on the draw and able to take out his targets quickly and effectively. Jonah is also a strong tracker and can follow a trail for days. Though he knows several different fighting styles and carries various weapons, he prefers a bare-knuckle brawl.

FUTURE FIGHTER
Jonah Hex was once mysteriously transported to the year 2050, where Earth was devastated by war and corruption. Hex was no stranger to the fight for freedom and soon found himself battling his way through the villains of the future. He eventually returned to the Old West.

105

THE JUSTICE LEAGUE OF AMERICA

THE WORLD'S GREATEST SUPER HEROES

When aliens from the planet Appellax targeted Earth for a takeover, the world's greatest heroes came together to defeat them as the Justice League of America. After the crisis, the JLA stayed together to defend the Earth against future threats. Many heroes have joined its ranks over the years. The JLA has seen its share of troubles and has been reborn several times under various leaders, but the team's commitment to peace and justice is as strong as ever.

HALL OF JUSTICE

The JLA's headquarters is the Hall of Justice, a majestic building in Washington, D.C. It houses a vast array of artifacts collected during the team's adventures. The JLA is able to teleport from the Hall to its orbiting space base, known as the Watchtower.

MEMBERS INCLUDE

Batman, Superman, Wonder Woman, Black Lightning, Zatanna, Arsenal, Vixen, Black Canary, The Flash, Green Lantern (Hal Jordan), Green Lantern (John Stewart), Red Tornado, Firestorm, Hawkgirl, Donna Troy,

THE JUSTICE SOCIETY OF AMERICA

THE WORLD'S FIRST SUPER-TEAM

The Justice Society of America was formed during World War II to combat Adolf Hitler's evil Nazi forces. The team defeated Hitler and restored freedom, but was then called before the nation and told that its members must give up their secret identities or retire. The JSA saw no other option but to disband and fade into normal life. Many years later, the team would reform, welcoming back original members to train the next generation of heroes.

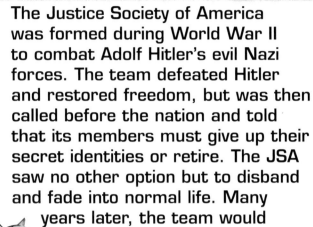

ALL-STARS
After a rift with the elder members of the Justice Society, the younger team members broke off and formed their own unit. Led by Power Girl, the new team featured Hourman, Stargirl, Atom-Smasher, Cyclone, and Anna Fortune. It was known as JSA All-Stars.

MEMBERS INCLUDE

Wildcat, The Flash (Jay Garrick), Liberty Belle, Doctor Mid-Nite, Mister America, Green Lantern (Alan Scott), Doctor Fate, Lightning, Obsidian, Power Girl, Cyclone, Tomcat, Mister America, Stargirl, Judomaster, King Chimera, Citizen Steel, Sandman, Atom-Smasher.

KARATE KID
MARTIAL ARTS MASTER

Karate Kid is a member of the Legion of Super-Heroes and an expert in the fighting styles of the past and future. Though fast on his feet, he's not always the quickest of his team to leap into action—he always looks for a peaceful way to victory first. Karate Kid uses his fighting skills only when he must!

VITAL STATS

REAL NAME Val Armorr
OCCUPATION Legionnaire
HEIGHT 5ft 8in
WEIGHT 160 lbs
BASE 31st century Earth
ALLIES Legion of Super-Heroes
FOES OMAC

Mental training makes him highly resistant to attempts at mind control.

He is able to sense his opponent's weakest spots and then target them.

COUNTDOWN

After a mission with the Legion to retrieve a special lightning rod, Karate Kid became stranded in the present day. While struggling to find a way back to the future, he was exposed to a rare version of the OMAC virus which left him incredibly sick.

POWERS: Karate Kid has mastered every fighting style in the galaxy, and is considered a living weapon. Although he knows many alien combat techniques, he prefers using classic martial arts from 20th century Earth. Karate Kid is also a good student with an exceptional eye for detail.

KATANA
SILENT SAMURAI

Katana wears a modified version of traditional samurai armor.

Katana's Soultaker Sword houses the spirits of the dead.

Her wrist gauntlets help her to deflect attacks.

Katana is an honorable samurai warrior from Japan. Her mission is to avenge the spirits of the dead. As a member of the heroic Outsiders team, she seeks out people who have been wronged and helps them find the justice they deserve. Katana can be shy at times, but her warrior spirit is strong.

VITAL STATS

REAL NAME Tatsu Yamashiro
OCCUPATION Hero
HEIGHT 5ft 2in
WEIGHT 118 lbs
BASE Markovia, Mobile
ALLIES The Outsiders, Batman
FOES Lady Shiva, Masters of Disaster

OUTSIDERS RETURN

When the Outsiders were on the verge of disbanding, Batman stepped in to mentor them once again. He tested each member to see if they had what it took to be a true hero. Katana passed with flying colors and was able to keep her place in the team.

POWERS: Katana is an accomplished martial artist and hand-to-hand fighter who is often underestimated because of her small size. Her sword, the Soultaker, captures the souls of everyone it strikes. Katana can communicate telepathically with the spirits inside it, although sometimes they try to negativel

KID FLASH
SUPER STREAK

Super-speed made baby Bart Allen grow too quickly, and his family took him from the future to the present to find a cure. Bart was lucky. His growth was slowed but not his speed, and he became Kid Flash. Bart is full of curiosity about the world around him and loves spending time with his friends, the Teen Titans.

VITAL STATS
REAL NAME Bart Allen
OCCUPATION Hero
HEIGHT 5ft 7in
WEIGHT 145 lbs
BASE San Francisco, Keystone City
ALLIES The Flash, Teen Titans, Superboy
FOES The Rogues, Inertia

A photographic memory enables him to recall everything he has seen or read.

Kid Flash's speed allows him to run on water.

MAX MERCURY
When Bart Allen first came to our time period he was taken in by Max Mercury, the oldest member of the Flash family and the very first speedster. Bart's impatience made him difficult to train, but Max was always supportive and encouraging.

POWERS: Kid Flash gets his power from the Speed Force, a powerful energy source that fuels all speedsters. He has yet to master his full abilities, but can run at super-speed, vibrate through solid objects, and create whirlwinds. Kid Flash has a thirst for knowledge and reads as many books as he can get his hands on.

KILLER CROC
REPTILIAN VILLAIN

Waylon Jones was born with a disease that made his skin green and scaly. He was rejected as a child because of his appearance, and grew up bitter and hostile. Now, as the monstrous criminal known as Killer Croc, he prowls the swamps of Gotham City, always looking to snap up his next victim.

His razor-sharp teeth are good for attacking and intimidating enemies.

Croc is protected by his coarse and leathery skin.

VITAL STATS
REAL NAME Waylon Jones
OCCUPATION Villain
HEIGHT 7ft 5in
WEIGHT 686 lbs
BASE Gotham City
ALLIES The Penguin, Hush
FOES Batman, Robin

POWERS: The beastly Killer Croc has incredible strength, stamina, and a vicious nature, which makes him one of Batman's fiercest foes. He also has enhanced senses which allow him to smell and stalk his prey. Croc might be big, but he lacks simple intelligence and is often manipulated by other villains.

EASY MONEY
Killer Croc's body further mutated, becoming even more reptilian. It caused him great agony. Croc thought that maybe money could buy him a cure, so he kidnapped the son of a wealthy businessman for a ransom. Thankfully, Batman rescued the boy, but Croc never found the cure he sought.

KILLER FROST
ICE QUEEN

Doctor Louise Lincoln blamed the hero Firestorm for the loss of her friend and mentor. Vowing to pay him back, she used her mentor's technology to gain superpowers and became Killer Frost. Despite being a foe of Firestorm, Frost seems to crave his attention and often commits crimes to get him to notice her.

VITAL STATS
REAL NAME Doctor Louise Lincoln
OCCUPATION Villain
HEIGHT 5ft 3in
WEIGHT 124 lbs
BASE Mobile
ALLIES Secret Society of Super-Villains
FOES Firestorm

Killer Frost can summon massive blizzards with a snap of her fingers.

When she gained her powers, her skin became a chilling shade of white.

FIRE AND ICE
Killer Frost was diagnosed with a fatal disease which also robbed her of her powers. In an attempt to save herself, she tricked Firestorm into curing her. As soon as Killer Frost's health and abilities were restored, the treacherous villain repaid her savior by attacking him.

POWERS: Killer Frost draws heat from any source, including the human body, leaving her victims frozen. This makes her chilling condition highly unstable. She's able to generate intense blasts of cold as well as sharp icicle-like projectiles. Killer Frost is also a brilliant doctor, even though she's evil.

KILOWOG

TOUGH TRAINER

Kilowog is an alien from the planet Bolovax Vik. His job is to train the new recruits of the Green Lantern Corps, and he takes it very seriously. Kilowog's students are often frightened by their drill instructor's hulking frame and booming voice, but they feel safe knowing he's fighting alongside them.

Using his power ring, Kilowog can create extraordinarily complex machinery.

Kilowog can link his mind with fellow Bolovaxians.

VITAL STATS

REAL NAME Kilowog
OCCUPATION Green Lantern
HEIGHT 8ft 3in
WEIGHT 720 lbs
BASE Oa
ALLIES John Stewart, Guy Gardner
FOES Sinestro

POWERS: Kilowog's Green Lantern ring can be used to create hard-light energy constructs (solid forms) and it helps him travel through space. His powerful build and years of training have made him a strong fighter. Kilowog is also a scientist, and his highly developed intellect helps him when pl

NEW RECRUIT

In his younger days, Kilowog was himself a Green Lantern recruit. His trainer was the tough-talking drill-instructor Lantern Ermey. Ermey was very hard on Kilowog for a reason: he knew that Kilowog possessed the strength and courage to become an exceptional Green Lantern

KRYPTO
SUPER-DOG

Krypto is Superman's dog. Just before the destruction of his home planet, Krypto was sent to Earth in a test rocket. There he was reunited with Superman, a.k.a. the young Clark Kent, who was growing up in the town of Smallville. Krypto works hard to please his master, but always seems to be getting into trouble.

VITAL STATS

REAL NAME Krypto
OCCUPATION Pet, Hero
HEIGHT 2ft 2in
WEIGHT 40 lbs
BASE Smallville, Mobile
ALLIES Superman, Superboy
FOES Lex Luthor, Brainiac

Krypto's senses are even more developed than those of an ordinary dog.

When he's not on duty, Krypto's cape is safely hidden under his collar.

SUPER-PROTECTIVE
Krypto's impulsive nature can make him slightly uncontrollable, even vicious at times—especially when it comes to protecting his master. When the demi-god Atlas attacked Superman, Krypto was on the front line, using all his strength to defend his best friend.

POWERS: Like Superman, Krypto gets his powers from the effects of Earth's yellow sun. They include flight, heat vision, and super-strength. He's an extremely loyal pet to the Kent family, but, because Krypto is a dog, he lacks the ability to control and understand his powers, and he often finds himself in over his head.

LADY BLACKHAWK
BEAUTIFUL BRAWLER

Lady Blackhawk's excellent hand-eye coordination makes her a top pilot.

Lady Blackhawk has been flying planes and fighting evil since the 1920s. At that time she was a member of the Blackhawks, a legendary team of pilots. After accidentally being transported forward in time to the present day, Lady Blackhawk was drafted by the hero Oracle to serve on the Birds of Prey team.

Lady Blackhawk's costume features the official Blackhawk insignia.

VITAL STATS
REAL NAME Zinda Blake
OCCUPATION Hero
HEIGHT 5ft 7in
WEIGHT 117 lbs
BASE Mobile
ALLIES Blackhawks, Birds of Prey
FOES Killer Shark, Spy Smasher

POWERS: Lady Blackhawk is strong in battle and has mastered many forms of hand-to-hand-combat, though she prefers basic street fighting. She is also an expert markswoman. Lady Blackhawk's flight training has made her an exceptional pilot with an understanding of both planes and helicopters.

ABLE AVIATOR
Lady Blackhawk is an expert with all types of aircraft and her skills have been put to the test countless times when rescuing her teammates from trouble areas. She can maneuver the Birds of Prey's state-of-the-art jet, the *Aerie One*, with no trouble at all.

LADY SHIVA
FATAL FIGHTER

Lady Shiva is one of the most lethal fighters on the planet and a cold-hearted assassin-for-hire. Her calculated, emotionless style makes her one of the most formidable enemies of the Birds of Prey super hero team. Shiva takes a special pleasure in defeating heroes she has helped to train herself.

VITAL STATS

REAL NAME Sandra Woosan
OCCUPATION Villain
HEIGHT 5ft 8in
WEIGHT 141 lbs
BASE Mobile
ALLIES League of Assassins
FOES Batman, Birds of Prey

Lady Shiva can read body language to predict when her opponent will strike.

She can control her body so that she feels no physical pain.

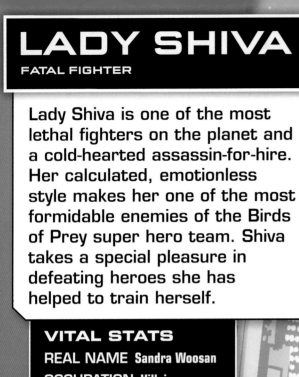

THE JADE CANARY
For a time, Lady Shiva replaced the hero Black Canary in the Birds of Prey so she could gain a better understanding of the nature of heroism. As the Jade Canary, Shiva assisted on various missions with the team before returning to her life of crime.

POWERS: Lady Shiva has mastered every known and forgotten martial art. She will go to any lengths to destroy her opponent in battle. Despite her villainous streak, Shiva holds a grudging respect for Earth's heroes. She has reluctantly trained many of them and continues to monitor them for weaknesses.

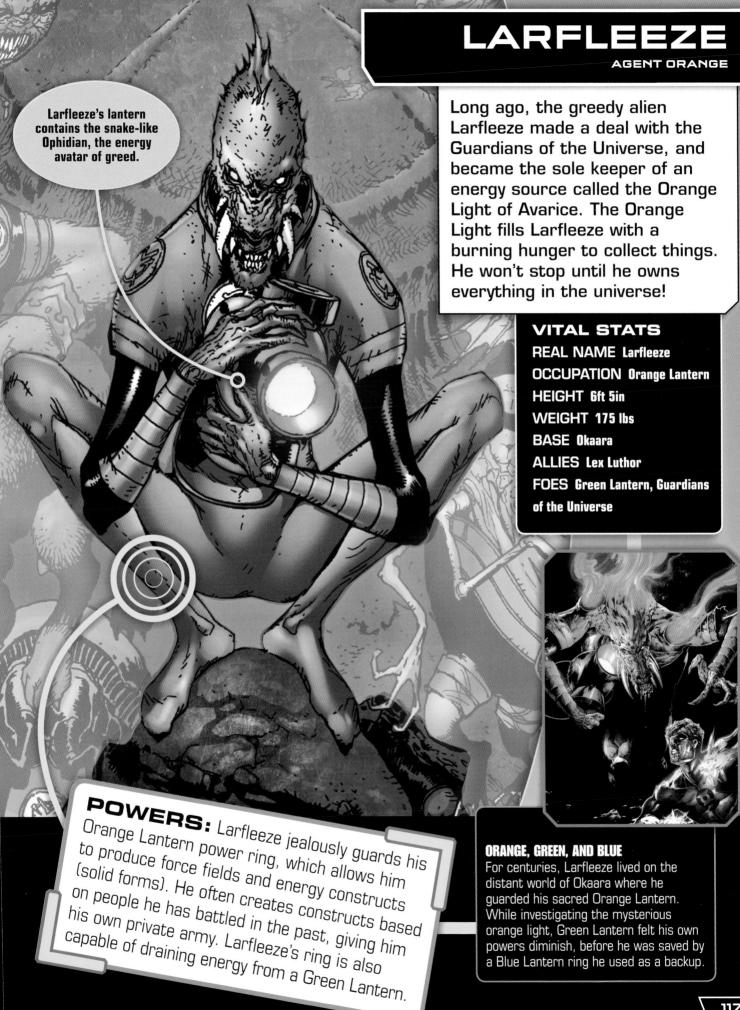

LARFLEEZE
AGENT ORANGE

Larfleeze's lantern contains the snake-like Ophidian, the energy avatar of greed.

Long ago, the greedy alien Larfleeze made a deal with the Guardians of the Universe, and became the sole keeper of an energy source called the Orange Light of Avarice. The Orange Light fills Larfleeze with a burning hunger to collect things. He won't stop until he owns everything in the universe!

VITAL STATS
REAL NAME Larfleeze
OCCUPATION Orange Lantern
HEIGHT 6ft 5in
WEIGHT 175 lbs
BASE Okaara
ALLIES Lex Luthor
FOES Green Lantern, Guardians of the Universe

POWERS: Larfleeze jealously guards his Orange Lantern power ring, which allows him to produce force fields and energy constructs (solid forms). He often creates constructs based on people he has battled in the past, giving him his own private army. Larfleeze's ring is also capable of draining energy from a Green Lantern.

ORANGE, GREEN, AND BLUE
For centuries, Larfleeze lived on the distant world of Okaara where he guarded his sacred Orange Lantern. While investigating the mysterious orange light, Green Lantern felt his own powers diminish, before he was saved by a Blue Lantern ring he used as a backup.

LEGION OF SUPER-HEROES

31ST CENTURY PROTECTORS

Inspired by the heroes of the past, the teenagers of the future fight for diversity and tolerance as the Legion of Super-Heroes! By the 31st century, many worlds had joined together under one government—the United Planets. Three superpowered teens saw a need for somebody to defend *all* the Planets, and so they founded the Legion. Its members, human and alien alike, have all sworn to protect the United Planets from any threat of danger.

R.J. BRANDE
Millionaire inventor R.J. Brande was saved from an assassin's bullet by Cosmic Boy, Saturn Girl,

MEMBERS INCLUDE
Ultra-Boy, Wildfire, Saturn Girl, Lightning Lad, Cosmic Boy, Brainiac 5, Dawnstar, Sensor Girl

LEX LUTHOR
CRIMINAL MASTERMIND

He uses much of his considerable brain power devising ways to defeat Superman.

Lex Luthor considers himself to be the most brilliant mind on Earth. He is driven by a need for power and uses his evil genius to try and destroy Superman, who constantly foils his plans for world domination. Luthor has been imprisoned many times, but somehow he always finds a way to escape.

VITAL STATS

REAL NAME Alexander Joseph Luthor

OCCUPATION Inventor, Villain

HEIGHT 6ft 2in

WEIGHT 210 lbs

BASE Metropolis

ALLIES Secret Society of Super-Villains, Injustice League

FOES Superman

Lex has traveled the world in search of the various shades of Kryptonite.

BATTLE-SUIT
As a criminal genius, Lex is constantly inventing new devices in his war against his nemesis Superman. To protect himself from Superman's powers in battle, Lex created a high-tech war suit made of impenetrable armor and equipped with Kryptonite lasers.

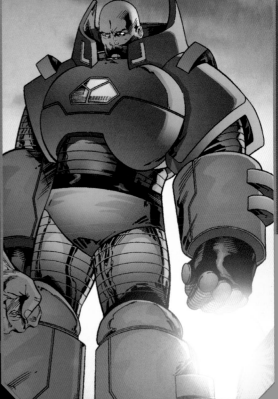

POWERS: Since he was a boy living in Smallville, Luthor has been a brilliant, self-taught scientist and inventor. He is also a skilled fighter and master manipulator. As an adult he created LexCorp, which specializes in innovative technologies, but instead of using his gifts to help humanity, Luthor pursues his own de...

LIBERTY BELLE

FREEDOM'S FURY

Jesse Chambers grew up in the shadow of her heroic parents, the original Liberty Belle and Johnny Quick. Choosing to honor their legacy, Jesse became a hero and fought alongside the Flash. Now going by the name Liberty Belle, in tribute to her mother, Jesse joined the famous Justice Society of America.

VITAL STATS

REAL NAME Jesse Belle Chambers

OCCUPATION Hero

HEIGHT 5ft 9in

WEIGHT 142 lbs

BASE Mobile

ALLIES The Flash, Justice Society of America

FOES Savitar, Icicle

The insignia on Liberty Belle's costume is the famous Liberty Bell.

Liberty Belle's costume was originally worn by her mother in World War II.

SUPER COUPLE

Liberty Belle is happily married to her Justice Society teammate, Hourman. Together they're the most famous couple in the super hero business. When the JSA was divided into different teams, Liberty Belle and Hourman made their marriage work, despite working apart.

POWERS: When Liberty Belle recites the formula "3x2(9YZ)4A," it gives her super-speed and agility, just as it did her father, Johnny Quick. Liberty Belle has slightly above-average strength and is a skilled fighter and ~~martial~~ artist. In her secret identity, she's also ~~...~~man and innovator.

LIGHTNING LAD
ELECTRIC LEGIONNAIRE

Lightning Lad is an electrically-powered hero from the planet Winath. He's a bit of a hothead and sometimes strikes without thinking, but his teammates in the Legion of Super-Heroes respect him for his honest opinions. Together with Cosmic Boy and Saturn Girl, he's a founding member of the team.

VITAL STATS
REAL NAME Garth Ranzz
OCCUPATION Legionnaire
HEIGHT 6ft 2in
WEIGHT 190 lbs
BASE 31st century Earth
ALLIES Legion of Super-Heroes
FOES Lightning Lord

Lightning Lad's body is not affected by his own electrical powers.

His tattoo depicts the Legion's symbol surrounded by lightning bolts.

POWERS: Lightning Lad can fire bolts of electrical energy from his fingertips. With this high-voltage power, he is capable of stunning or destroying his opponents. He can also fly using his Legion-issued flight ring. Lightning Lad is a strong fighter, and can be impulsive in battle although he works hard at controlling himself.

SATURN GIRL'S SWEETHEART
As a teenager, Lightning Lad harbored a huge crush on his Legion teammate, Saturn Girl. As well as doing his best to protect Saturn Girl in battle, Lightning Lad would often try to impress her by staging elaborate displays of power in the hope that she would fall in love with him. His plan eventually worked, and the two later married.

121

LOBO
ANGRY ALIEN

Lobo is the last survivor of the planet Czarnia and one of the most hated and feared bounty hunters in the galaxy. He's rude, crude, and plays by his own rules, which makes him a real danger to preservers of justice. Lobo is a frequent thorn in the side of Superman and the Justice League of America.

Lobo's stark white skin and piercing red eyes are the mark of a Czarnian.

His exceptional sense of smell enables him to track objects across the solar system.

VITAL STATS

REAL NAME Unpronounceable
OCCUPATION Villain
HEIGHT 7ft 6in
WEIGHT 640 lbs
BASE Space
ALLIES R.E.B.E.L.S.
FOES Superman

RENEGADE BIKER
Lobo is a bounty hunter who does not give up! He chases his prey across the universe on his giant motorbike, which has never let him down. With his trusty bulldog companion Dawg by his side and a varied collection of deadly weapons, Lobo is a force to be reckoned with.

POWERS: Lobo is indestructible: he can regenerate his entire body from a single drop of blood. He has super-strength and speed, and is a brutish fighter. As a bounty hunter, Lobo can track anyone across the galaxy. Although he hires himself out for money, he enjoys the thrill of the hunt and the pleasure of the kill.

LOIS LANE
STAR REPORTER

Lois Lane is the *Daily Planet's* star reporter, and she will do whatever it takes to get her story. Like her father, an army general, Lois is very stubborn. Her determination to do her job well often gets her into dangerous situations, but thankfully Superman is always there to protect her.

Her trusty tape recorder helps her to remember all the details for her stories.

Lois's press pass gives her access to important people.

PRESS
LANE . LOIS

VITAL STATS

REAL NAME Lois Joanne Lane
OCCUPATION Reporter
HEIGHT 5ft 6in
WEIGHT 136 lbs
BASE Metropolis
ALLIES Superman
FOES Lex Luthor

POWERS: Lois is an accomplished investigative journalist with a passion for the truth. She knows when a story is important, and strives to present the facts as clearly as possible, though her strong opinions shine through from time to time. Lois is a solid hand-to-hand combatant and

A GREAT METROPOLITAN NEWSPAPER
Lois Lane is a Pulitzer Prize winning journalist. She thought she was the best reporter at the *Daily Planet* until Clark Kent showed up. At first she wasn't impressed by Clark's investigative skills, but after reading his stories she realized that a little healthy competition wouldn't be a bad thing.

MAD HATTER
FAIRYTALE FIEND

The Mad Hatter is one of the most dangerous criminals in Gotham City. He and his Wonderland Gang often torment Batman with their fairytale-based crimes. But there's never a happy ending for Hatter. He always ends up in Arkham Asylum, Gotham's hospital for the criminally insane.

VITAL STATS

REAL NAME Jervis Tetch

OCCUPATION Villain

HEIGHT 4ft 8in

WEIGHT 149 lbs

BASE Gotham City

ALLIES Secret Six, Doctor Psycho

FOES Batman, Robin

The Mad Hatter is lost without his favorite top hat.

His ghastly appearance frightens friends and foes alike.

BETRAYED BY THE SIX
The Mad Hatter was recruited by the group of criminals known as the Secret Six because of his ability to manipulate minds. However, he was later betrayed by his teammate Ragdoll, who pushed him off a rooftop. Hatter vowed to destroy the Six but has yet to see his vengeance realized.

POWERS: Mad Hatter is a master hypnotist who uses his skills to invade people's minds. Hatter uses chemicals and electronics, disguised within special hats, to control his victims. Because of his short stature, the Mad ... a very good fighter, and prefers to ... for him.

MAN-BAT
NOCTURNAL NIGHTMARE

His leathery, bat-like wings allow him to fly.

Doctor Kirk Langstrom created a special serum, based on the sonar abilities of bats, in an attempt to cure his hearing loss. But it transformed him into a monstrous bat creature that terrorized the skies over Gotham City. At first, Langstrom could control his powers, but now he's hopelessly addicted to the serum!

VITAL STATS
REAL NAME Doctor Kirk Langstrom

OCCUPATION Biologist

HEIGHT 7ft 4in

WEIGHT 315 lbs

BASE Gotham City

ALLIES League of Assassins, Talia al Ghul

FOES Batman

Man-Bat has sharp claws and teeth.

POWERS: After drinking the serum, Langstrom becomes a giant bat-like creature with super-strength and endurance. He has all the special abilities of a bat, including flight, sonar, and enhanced night vision—but he can become extremely volatile too. Langstrom often loses his memory while in his transformed

KIRK LANGSTROM
Kirk Langstrom is a respected scientist, and has worked diligently through the years to find a cure for his terrible affliction. Other villains, such as Talia al Ghul, envy Langstrom's abilities and have attempted to use the formula for their own nefarious purposes.

MANHUNTER
DEFENDER OF JUSTICE

Lawyer Kate Spencer hated seeing criminals go unpunished, so when she found a stash of secret weapons she put them to good use and became the heroic Manhunter! By day, Kate helps put criminals away in her role as a lawyer. At night, she joins the Birds of Prey team in the pursuit of justice.

VITAL STATS

REAL NAME Katherine "Kate" Spencer

OCCUPATION District Attorney, Hero

HEIGHT 5ft 8in

WEIGHT 145 lbs

BASE Gotham City

ALLIES Birds of Prey, Cameron Chase

FOES Copperhead, Phobia

She wears clawed wrist gauntlets.

Manhunter uses a powerful staff capable of firing energy blasts.

IN THE NAME OF THE LAW

As an attorney, Kate was frustrated with the judicial system that saw many powerful criminals mistakenly released. She now works in Gotham City as the District Attorney alongside Commissioner Gordon. Together they strive

POWERS: Manhunter's red suit once belonged to a galactic police force known as the Darkstars, so it is made of a protective material. She is a skilled athlete and fighter and continues to push herself to the limit in her ... is also incredibly intelligent

MARTIAN MANHUNTER
SOLE SURVIVOR

His Martian vision allows him to project laser beams from his eyes.

Martian Manhunter lost his family when a terrible plague struck his home planet of Mars. Then, while still grieving, he was accidentally transported to Earth. Unable to return, Manhunter tried his best to fit in among humans, joining the Justice League of America. His teammates consider him a good friend and wise comrade.

VITAL STATS
REAL NAME J'onn J'onzz/ John Jones
OCCUPATION Hero
HEIGHT 6ft 7in
WEIGHT 300 lbs
BASE Earth, Mars
ALLIES Justice League of America
FOES D'Kay, Malefic

He is a shape-shifter—able to take on any form he chooses.

FERNUS ATTACKS
Ever since he saw his planet consumed by flames, Martian Manhunter has had a fear of fire. An attempt to cure himself of this weakness left his mind fragmented and released an evil alter-ego named Fernus. Fernus was later destroyed, and Manhunter was freed from his phobia.

POWERS: Martian Manhunter has a variety of powers including super-strength, super-speed, and invisibility. He's thought to be as strong as or possibly stronger than Superman. Manhunter has highly developed telepathic powers and frequently uses them to link the minds of his Justice League teammates.

METAL MEN
AMAZING ANDROIDS

The Metal Men are a team of robots created by Doctor Will Magnus. Each is made from a different metal and programmed with a different personality based on the element they represent. They can all morph their bodies into any shape. The Metal Men sometimes argue, but they remain the best of friends.

MEMBERS INCLUDE

1 MERCURY Mercury's body is liquid at room temperature, making him quite unpredictable.

2 TIN Tin is slightly insecure but his teammates can always depend on him in battle.

3 PLATINUM Platinum has a crush on Doctor Magnus and considers herself the glamorous member of the group.

4 IRON Iron is super-strong and serves as the group's most durable member.

5 DOCTOR WILL MAGNUS Magnus created a device called the Responsometer which brought the Metal Men to life.

6 GOLD Gold serves as the team's noble leader and can stretch his body into any shape.

7 LEAD Lead may not be the smartest Metal Man, but he makes up for it by having a big heart.

8 COPPER Copper is the newest member of the team. She fits right in with her sarcastic personality.

ALLOY
The Metal Men were once brainwashed by the villainous businessman Maxwell Lord, who sent them to destroy the Justice League. During the battle they merged into a giant creature called Alloy, but were defeated by the JLA heroes and released from Lord's mind control.

METALLO
ARMORED ADVERSARY

John Corben was a respected member of the U.S. Army until Lex Luthor drafted him for a top secret project designed to take down Superman. When Corben was injured in action, Luthor replaced his heart with deadly Kryptonite. Corben became a criminal bent on revenge against Superman—and Metallo was born!

VITAL STATS
REAL NAME John Corben
OCCUPATION Criminal
HEIGHT 6ft 2in
WEIGHT 310 lbs
BASE Metropolis
ALLIES Lex Luthor
FOES Superman

If Metallo's Kryptonite heart is removed, he will die.

Metallo's streamlined armor protects him from attack.

POWERS: Metallo originally wore a huge suit of armor which gave him super-strength. But he doesn't need it anymore. Now, with his Kryptonite heart, Metallo himself is lethal to Superman and can destroy him in minutes. Because of his army training, Metallo is a smart tactician who enjoys the thrill of battle.

KRYPTONITE KILLS
Lex Luthor placed a variety of Kryptonite pieces inside Metallo, each possessing a different ability. Red Kryptonite can alter Superman's powers while gold Kryptonite can take them away. Together, Luthor and Metallo formed the Superman Revenge Squad alongside Bizarro and the Parasite.

METAMORPHO
THE ELEMENT MAN

Rex Mason was an archaeologist who was always searching for adventure. When he came across a mystical meteor called the Orb of Ra, it transformed him into the superpowered Metamorpho. Now he fights evil as part of the Outsiders super hero team. His optimistic attitude makes him popular with his teammates.

VITAL STATS

REAL NAME Rex Mason
OCCUPATION Adventurer, Hero
HEIGHT 6ft 1in
WEIGHT 200 lbs
BASE Mobile
ALLIES The Outsiders, Justice League of America
FOES Simon Stagg

Metamorpho can morph his body into a weapon to defend himself.

Metamorpho's mineral body appears as a variety of colors.

THE STAGG FAMILY
Billionaire Simon Stagg hired Rex Mason to find the Orb of Ra. Stagg wanted the Orb for himself and was angered when he lost its power to Mason. Stagg's daughter Sapphire later fell in love with Mason against her father's wishes.

POWERS: Metamorpho has the ability to become any element he chooses. He can make himself hard as a diamond, glow bright like phosphorus, or become a burst of steam. He can transform into any chemical combination imaginable. Metamorpho is also a versatile shape-shifter and mimic.

Metron's Mobius Chair enables him to travel through time, space, and alternate dimensions.

Metron is one of the New Gods. He travels the universe in his Mobius Chair, observing human affairs. He prefers to watch events, rather than participating in and influencing them. Metron's intentions are fairly benevolent, though he has occasionally been known to pit heroes against each other for sport.

VITAL STATS

REAL NAME None

OCCUPATION Explorer

HEIGHT 6ft 1in

WEIGHT 190 lbs

BASE New Genesis

ALLIES The New Gods

FOES Darkseid

The Mobius Chair is powered by the mysterious X Element.

POWERS: Metron is a scientific genius and he prefers to study humans rather than engage them. He can be cold and calculating and will usually shy away from combat situations. Though the New Gods respect Metron and his intelligence, they are often left wondering what his next move will be.

THE SOURCE WALL
Metron is one of the few beings who know the location of the Source Wall at the farthest edge of the universe. Beyond the Source Wall lies the Source, the secret to life. Many have tried to unlock this great secret but have ultimately been trapped in the Wall as a warning to future seekers.

MIRROR MASTER
REFLECTION OF EVIL

Evan McCulloch is a villain-for-hire who pursues a life of crime as the Mirror Master. If the price is right, Mirror Master will do any job he's offered. He prefers to work alone but is also a member of the Flash's Rogues Gallery of enemies, where he causes mayhem alongside Tar Pit and the Trickster.

VITAL STATS

REAL NAME Evan McCulloch

OCCUPATION Villain

HEIGHT 5ft 11in

WEIGHT 173 lbs

BASE Keystone City

ALLIES The Rogues

FOES The Flash, Animal Man

THE ROGUES
Mirror Master knows there is strength in numbers, and has teamed up with the villainous group, the Rogues. The Rogues follow a strict code to prevent members from getting out of line. Though many apply for membership, only a select few are accepted into this evil club.

Mirror Master uses two mirror guns that shoot lasers.

POWERS: Mirror Master can hide in any reflective surface and uses mirrors to commit his crimes. He has an arsenal of reflective weaponry, some of which can open portals to alternate dimensions, where he can transport his enemies. He enjoys the good life and often spends his stolen riches on expensive things.

MISTER FREEZE
FROSTY FIEND

Victor Fries was a scientist whose wife was stricken with a terrible disease. In order to save her life, Victor began working for GothCorp, but a terrible accident destroyed the cryogenic capsule she was kept in and she lost her life. Seeking vengeance against GothCorp, Victor became the cold-hearted Mister Freeze.

VITAL STATS
REAL NAME Victor Fries
OCCUPATION Criminal
HEIGHT 6ft
WEIGHT 190 lbs
BASE Gotham City
ALLIES Secret Society of Super-Villains
FOES Batman

Without his cryo-suit, Freeze would die.

He carries a powerful freezing gun.

CHILLING LOSS
Before his transformation into Mister Freeze, Victor Fries was a successful scientist who was happy with his life. He was very much in love with his wife Nora, and enjoyed sharing his work with her. After Nora's death, Victor was left a sad, broken man.

POWERS: Mister Freeze is a gifted scientist with an incredible mind for invention. His fascination with cryogenics dates back to his childhood when he liked to freeze animals. When his employers at GothCorp uncovered his misuse of company money to cure his wife, Victor was injured, resulting in his current state.

MISTER MIRACLE
THE WORLD'S GREATEST ESCAPE ARTIST

Mister Miracle was raised in the firepits of the planet Apokolips but eventually escaped and fled to New Genesis, where he joined the benevolent New Gods. Later, Miracle and his wife, Big Barda, made their home on Earth where Miracle often serves with the Justice League of America.

His cape can encase him in a cocoon and shield him from attacks.

VITAL STATS
REAL NAME Scott Free
OCCUPATION Hero
HEIGHT 6ft
WEIGHT 185 lbs
BASE New Genesis
ALLIES Big Barda, Orion
FOES Darkseid

GREAT ESCAPES
When Scott Free first came to Earth, he joined the circus. His trainer was an escape artist called Thaddeus Brown who performed under the stage name Mister Miracle. Later, Scott would take his mentor's name and use his skills as an escape artist to fight against evil.

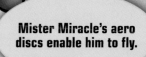

Mister Miracle's aero discs enable him to fly.

POWERS: Mister Miracle is a master escape artist and there's no trap that can hold him. He's also an exceptional athlete and hand-to-hand fighter. As a genius inventor, Mister Miracle has created a variety of complicated weapons, among them his multi-cube which fires laser beams and sonic blasts.

MISTER MXYZPTLK

DEVILISH IMP

Mister Mxyzptlk is a trickster from the 5th Dimension who loves to torment Superman with practical jokes. Mxy is very powerful and his special brand of magic has been known to make the Man of Steel powerless. The only way to defeat the formidable imp is to get him to say his name backwards.

Mister Mxyzptlk can alter his appearance to fool Superman.

VITAL STATS

REAL NAME Untranslatable

OCCUPATION Villain

HEIGHT 3ft 9in

WEIGHT 59 lbs

BASE The 5th Dimension

ALLIES Bat-Mite

FOES Superman

EMPEROR JOKER

The Joker once tricked Mxyzptlk into giving him his powers, and the entire world was erased and remade in the Joker's evil image. Thankfully, Mxyzptlk was able to snap out of his trance and convince Superman to save the world once again.

POWERS: There are virtually no limits to Mxyzptlk's magical powers, which include shape-changing and mind control. Superman is at the mercy of almost anything Mxy's warped mind can think of. Though he generally wants to cause simple mischief, Mxyzptlk has been known to have a nasty streak.

MISTER TERRIFIC
THE SMARTEST MAN ON EARTH

Michael Holt was the best at everything: the best student, the best Olympic athlete, and the best husband. After a freak accident took his wife, Michael decided to become the best hero he could be. As Mister Terrific, he has devoted his life to the pursuit of justice and the principle of equality for all.

Terrific controls his T-Spheres using a mask and earpiece.

VITAL STATS
REAL NAME Michael Holt
OCCUPATION Hero
HEIGHT 6ft 2in
WEIGHT 215 lbs
BASE New York City
ALLIES Justice Society of America, Checkmate
FOES Roulette, Amanda Waller

T-Spheres shield Terrific from detection by any kind of technology.

BLEEEP

T-SPHERES
Mister Terrific invented a device called a T-Sphere which can create holograms, project beams of light, and enable long distance communication. It can also gather information and spy on Mister Terrific's enemies. Terrific has many T-Spheres, and often sends them on multiple missions at once.

POWERS: Mister Terrific is a genius who has mastered various maths, sciences, and languages. He is an excellent athlete and is always in peak physical condition thanks to his intense Olympic training. Mister Terrific is also a skilled fighter and is skilled in many martial arts.

MON-EL
DAXAMITE HERO

X-ray vision enables Mon-El to see through solid objects.

Mon-El is a powerful hero from the planet Daxam and a proud member of the Legion of Super-Heroes. He's also one of Superman's closest friends—in fact, the Man of Steel considers Mon-El a brother. Mon-El once even traveled to the past and helped to defend Metropolis against villains during Superman's absence.

Mon-El was recently made the sole Green Lantern of the 31st century.

VITAL STATS

REAL NAME Lar Gand
OCCUPATION Legionnaire
HEIGHT 6ft 2in
WEIGHT 200 lbs
BASE 31st century Earth
ALLIES Superman, Legion of Super-Heroes
FOES General Zod, Brainiac

POWERS: Earth's yellow sun gives Mon-El many powers, including super-strength, super-hearing, invulnerability, flight, heat vision, and freezing breath. Mon-El's body chemistry is very similar to Superman's, but whereas Superman can be weakened by Kryptonite, Mon-El is weakened by lead.

TRAPPED IN THE ZONE
Mon-El was once poisoned by lead—an element that can weaken and kill Daxamites. A young Superman was forced to send him into the prison dimension known as the Phantom Zone to keep him alive until a cure could be found. Mon-El had to endure centuries in the dark Kryptonian prison before he was freed.

MONGUL
RULER OF WARWORLD

Mongul is a ruthless warlord who seeks to conquer the universe one planet at a time. Recently, Mongul appointed himself leader of the villainous Sinestro Corps. He has made it clear to Sinestro—the former leader—that no one will stand in Mongul's way of total world domination!

VITAL STATS

REAL NAME Mongul
OCCUPATION Warlord
HEIGHT 7ft 9in
WEIGHT 1,135 lbs
BASE Warworld
ALLIES Cyborg Superman, Imperiex
FOES Superman, Green Lantern

His powerful harness allows him to project lethal blasts of energy from his chest.

Mongul's immense size and bulk make him a threat to all who oppose him.

CHALLENGING SINESTRO CORPS
Mongul defeated a Sinestro Corps member in battle and received a yellow power ring as his prize. Recognizing an opportunity to gain more power, Mongul began tracking down all the Sinestro Corps members and destroying those who refused to serve under his rule.

POWERS: Mongul has super-strength and his rock-like body makes him invulnerable to harm. He is also able to regenerate body parts quickly. When armed with his power ring he's capable of creating yellow energy constructs with his mind. Mongul has a thirst for power and enjoys using brute force against foes.

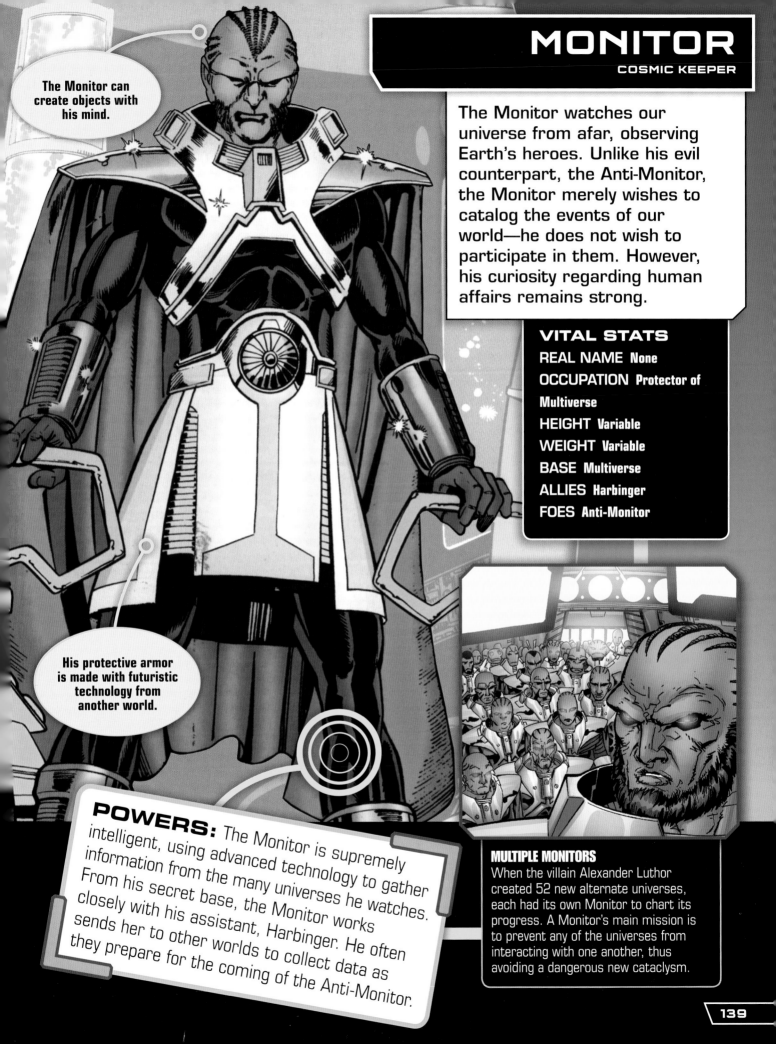

The Monitor can create objects with his mind.

MONITOR
COSMIC KEEPER

The Monitor watches our universe from afar, observing Earth's heroes. Unlike his evil counterpart, the Anti-Monitor, the Monitor merely wishes to catalog the events of our world—he does not wish to participate in them. However, his curiosity regarding human affairs remains strong.

VITAL STATS
REAL NAME None
OCCUPATION Protector of Multiverse
HEIGHT Variable
WEIGHT Variable
BASE Multiverse
ALLIES Harbinger
FOES Anti-Monitor

His protective armor is made with futuristic technology from another world.

POWERS: The Monitor is supremely intelligent, using advanced technology to gather information from the many universes he watches. From his secret base, the Monitor works closely with his assistant, Harbinger. He often sends her to other worlds to collect data as they prepare for the coming of the Anti-Monitor.

MULTIPLE MONITORS
When the villain Alexander Luthor created 52 new alternate universes, each had its own Monitor to chart its progress. A Monitor's main mission is to prevent any of the universes from interacting with one another, thus avoiding a dangerous new cataclysm.

MONSIEUR MALLAH

BRAIN TRUST

Monsieur Mallah was an ordinary gorilla until a mad scientist's experiment gave him human intelligence. After the scientist died, his brain was placed into a special device, allowing him to communicate with Mallah. Together, Mallah and the diabolical Brain formed the Brotherhood of Evil.

VITAL STATS

REAL NAME None
OCCUPATION Villain
HEIGHT 6ft 3in
WEIGHT 345 lbs
BASE Mobile
ALLIES Brotherhood of Evil
FOES Teen Titans, Doom Patrol

The Brain is kept in a protective device that nourishes it with chemicals.

Mallah is equipped with many weapons, including a large, powerful gun.

GORILLA WARFARE

When the villains of Earth were sent to a new prison on the alien world Cygnus 4019, tensions ran high. Monsieur Mallah reached out to fellow ape Gorilla Grodd in the hope that they might work together to return home, but instead Grodd attacked!

POWERS: Monsieur Mallah has above-average strength and agility due to his gorilla body. He possesses human-level intelligence, and can speak several languages, including English and French. Mallah obeys the Brain at all times, and will do anything he says. The two have yet to conquer the world.

THE NEW GODS
HEROES OF NEW GENESIS

Centuries ago, a mysterious force called the Godwave split apart the cosmos, dividing the Old Gods' world into two new planets. Apokolips became the home of the tyrannical Darkseid and his evil minions, and on New Genesis dwelt the New Gods. Some of the New Gods are kind, and have assisted the heroes of Earth in numerous battles over the years.

HIGHFATHER
The immortal Highfather is the chief of the New Gods and ruler of New Genesis. He carries a power staff and is able to communicate directly with the Source, a mystical energy that holds the secret to life. Darkseid hates Highfather, and wishes he himself had access to the Source.

THE NEW GODS INCLUDE
Kalibak, Doctor Bedlam, Big Barda, Serifin, Mantis, Takion, Black Racer, Kanto, Orion, Infinity Man, Beautiful Dreamer, Big Bear, Himon, Granny Goodness, Mister Miracle, Vermin Vunderbar, Desaad

NIGHTWING
WONDER OF THE NIGHT

Dick Grayson began his crime fighting career as Robin, the Boy Wonder. A skilled acrobat and fighter, Dick later moved out from under Batman's shadow to become a new hero called Nightwing. Nightwing is known for his daring courage, and he serves as a respected mentor to the Teen Titans.

VITAL STATS

REAL NAME Richard "Dick" Grayson

OCCUPATION Hero

HEIGHT 5ft 10in

WEIGHT 175 lbs

BASE Gotham City

ALLIES Batman, Robin

FOES Two-Face, Blockbuster

His wrist and boot gauntlets contain smoke pellets, flares, and other items.

Nightwing uses Escrima fighting sticks to defend himself.

FRIENDS FOREVER
During his younger years, Dick Grayson harbored a crush on the first Batgirl, Barbara Gordon, who later became known as Oracle. As the two heroes reached adulthood, their relationship grew stronger through tragedy and triumph. Now as friends, they value each other more than ever.

POWERS: Nightwing's childhood experiences as a circus acrobat and trapeze artist make him extremely agile. He is a superior fighter and has been trained by Batman and the Teen Titans in many forms of self-defense. ... a keen detective, and is driven ... ame of justice.

Obsidian can telepathically force people to see the evil side of their soul.

As a child, Todd Rice found that he was able to communicate with shadows. He transformed himself into the powerful hero Obsidian in order to control the dark energies growing stronger inside him. Together with his twin sister, Jade, Obsidian now protects the mystical power source known as the Starheart.

VITAL STATS
REAL NAME Todd Rice
OCCUPATION Hero
HEIGHT 5ft 11in
WEIGHT 193 lbs
BASE Mobile
ALLIES Justice Society of America, Jade
FOES Ian Karkull, Eclipso

Obsidian surrounds himself with the dark mists of the Shadowlands.

POWERS: Obsidian can manipulate shadow forces and transport people to a place called the Shadowlands where their fears come to life. He also possesses super-strength and is able to fly, thanks to the power of the Starheart. Because they're twins, Obsidian and Jade have a low-level telepathic link with each other.

BLACK EGG
Obsidian was once turned into a powerful black egg by a group of villains. The villains planned to use the egg to power a Darkness Engine that would remove the powers of every super hero on Earth. Fortunately, Obsidian eventually broke free and saved the world.

OCEAN MASTER

DEVIL OF THE DEPTHS

Ocean Master is an underwater wizard and the villainous half-brother of Aquaman. He seethes with jealousy toward Aquaman, and has been banished from the kingdom of Atlantis. Ocean Master sold his soul to the demon, Neron, in exchange for more power and is currently plotting his brother's demise.

VITAL STATS

REAL NAME Orm Marius
OCCUPATION Villain
HEIGHT 5ft 11in
WEIGHT 200 lbs
BASE Atlantis
ALLIES Black Manta
FOES Aquaman

A protective helmet allows Ocean Master to breathe underwater.

Beneath his mask, Ocean Master's face is horribly scarred.

He experiences intense pain if he is separated from his powerful trident.

BROTHERLY HATE

Ocean Master sees himself as the true King of Atlantis and will stop at nothing to destroy Aquaman's life. Once, he even altered reality with his magical powers in order to crown himself king. But his plans were thwarted by his arch nemesis and the true king, Aquaman.

POWERS: Ocean Master is able to breathe underwater and can swim at great speeds. His body is also able to withstand ocean pressures. Ocean Master is a highly skilled magician and his trident possesses many mystical abilities, including illusion-casting and energy blasting.

The symbol on an OMAC's chest represents the all-seeing Brother Eye satellite.

OMAC
OMNI MIND AND COMMUNITY

When Batman created a spy satellite to monitor heroes and villains, he never imagined it would fall into the hands of evil businessman Maxwell Lord! Max used the satellite, called Brother Eye, to infect millions of humans with a cybernetic virus. It turned each of them into a robotic destroyer known as an OMAC.

An OMAC has the ability to grow to an enormous size.

VITAL STATS
REAL NAME Inapplicable
OCCUPATION Cybernetic Virus
HEIGHT Variable
WEIGHT Variable
BASE Mobile
ALLIES Maxwell Lord
FOES Superman

POWERS: Once the OMAC virus infects its host, it is virtually unstoppable. Each OMAC has incredible super-strength and speed, as well as the ability to fly. An OMAC can also fire destructive energy blasts at opponents. When clustered in a group, numerous OMAC units can quickly become an overwhelming force.

OMAC ARMY
Maxwell Lord made arrangements for more than a million OMAC units to go into action in the event of his death. As the robotic renegades attacked Earth's heroes, Batman led a small group to destroy the Brother Eye satellite, which was controlling the OMAC army.

ORACLE

INFORMATION CENTRAL

Barbara Gordon is Commissioner Gordon's daughter. She was once Batgirl, protecting the night skies over Gotham City, but an injury left her paralyzed. Now, as Oracle, she uses information as her weapon. With her vast computer network, Oracle is linked up to every hero on the planet and is always ready to help.

VITAL STATS

REAL NAME Barbara Gordon
OCCUPATION Hero
HEIGHT 5ft 11in
WEIGHT 148 lbs
BASE Gotham City
ALLIES Birds of Prey, Batman, Robin
FOES The Joker, Spy Smasher

Oracle has a brilliant mind and a flawless memory.

She conceals a variety of weapons in her wheelchair.

BATGIRL

When Batman and Robin first appeared in Gotham City, young Barbara dreamed of fighting crime alongside them. The super-smart teenager completed high school early and became Batgirl. During her years as the caped hero, she took on many of Batman's fiercest enemies.

POWERS: With a photographic memory, Oracle is considered information central in the super hero community. She is a computer specialist and expert hacker—and she has files on every villain and hero. Oracle is also a skilled hand-to-hand fighter and is experienced in many diverse forms of weaponry.

ORION
THE HUNTER

Orion's astro-glider protects him from the harshness of space travel.

Orion is a proud warrior of the planet New Genesis. He has chosen the life of a hero, but finds it a constant struggle to control the fiery temper he inherited from his father, the villainous Darkseid. Orion teams up with the Justice League on occasion, where his warrior's instinct is put to good use.

VITAL STATS
REAL NAME Orion
OCCUPATION Warrior, Hero
HEIGHT 6ft 1in
WEIGHT 195 lbs
BASE New Genesis
ALLIES Mister Miracle, Lightray
FOES Darkseid, Kalibak

The astro-glider fires concussive blasts and enables Orion to travel between dimensions.

POWERS: Orion is an immortal being who possesses enormous strength, speed, and stamina. He also has a healing factor that allows him to recover quickly from injury. Orion is a fierce and sometimes brutish fighter who is skilled at hunting down his enemies and bringing them to justice.

MOTHER BOX
Orion possesses a device called a Mother Box, a living computer from New Genesis whose properties include teleportation, energy manipulation, and the ability to heal. Orion's Mother Box performs the difficult task of keeping his uncontrollable rage in check.

THE OUTSIDERS
OUTSIDE THE LAW

The Outsiders were formed by Batman to handle the toughest tasks that other heroes might find too difficult. There's no mission the Outsiders won't undertake to protect those in need. Recently, the team's ranks have been divided, with Geo-Force and Black Lightning vying for leadership.

MEMBERS INCLUDE

1 KATANA Tatsu Yamashiro uses her mystical sword, the Soultaker, to defend the innocent.

2 GEO-FORCE Prince Brion of Markovia is the leader of the Outsiders. He has control over the Earth itself.

3 METAMORPHO Rex Mason's body was changed by the ancient Orb of Ra, and he found he could transform himself into the elements of the Earth.

4 THE CREEPER Jack Ryder is a sensationalist TV reporter who turns into the freakishly frightening Creeper.

5 OWLMAN Detective Roy Raymond Jr. uses his keen detective skills to solve mysteries as Owlman.

6 BLACK LIGHTNING Teacher Jefferson Pierce uses his high-voltage electrical powers to fight injustice.

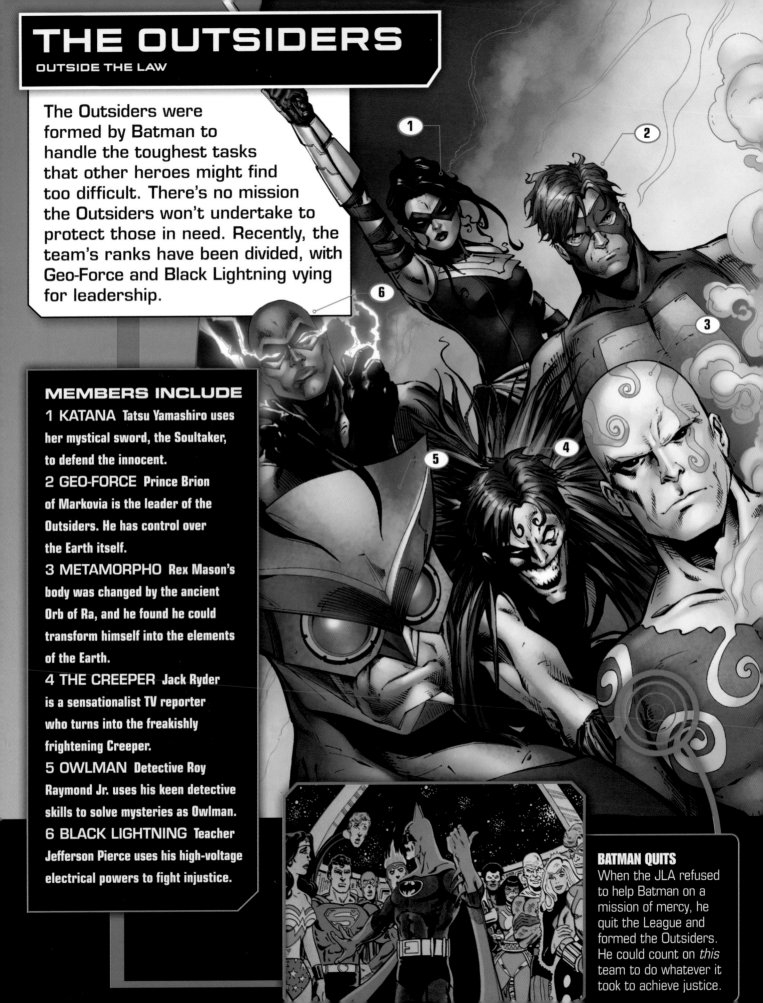

BATMAN QUITS
When the JLA refused to help Batman on a mission of mercy, he quit the League and formed the Outsiders. He could count on *this* team to do whatever it took to achieve justice.

PARALLAX
THE POWER OF FEAR

Parallax is a mystical energy creature who gains power from the emotion of fear. The Guardians of the Universe kept him hostage for centuries, worried that he would corrupt their Green Lantern Corps. Now free, Parallax uses his fearsome energy to fuel the Lanterns' rival group, the evil Sinestro Corps.

On the emotional spectrum, fear is associated with the color yellow.

Parallax began life as a small insect on prehistoric Earth.

VITAL STATS
REAL NAME Parallax
OCCUPATION Fear Entity
HEIGHT Undetermined
WEIGHT Undetermined
BASE Mobile
ALLIES Sinestro
FOES Green Lantern Corps, Guardians of the Universe

POWERS:
Parallax is the embodiment of fear who seeks out host bodies to corrupt. When Parallax senses that a host body feels fear or self-doubt, he strikes, entering that body and taking control. Parallax is immortal and has virtually unlimited abilities that include mind control and energy manipulation.

POSSESSED
Parallax has taken control of many people over the years, but he most craves the power he can wield when in control of a Green Lantern. Both Hal Jordan and Kyle Rayner have struggled to control their actions while being possessed by Parallax.

149

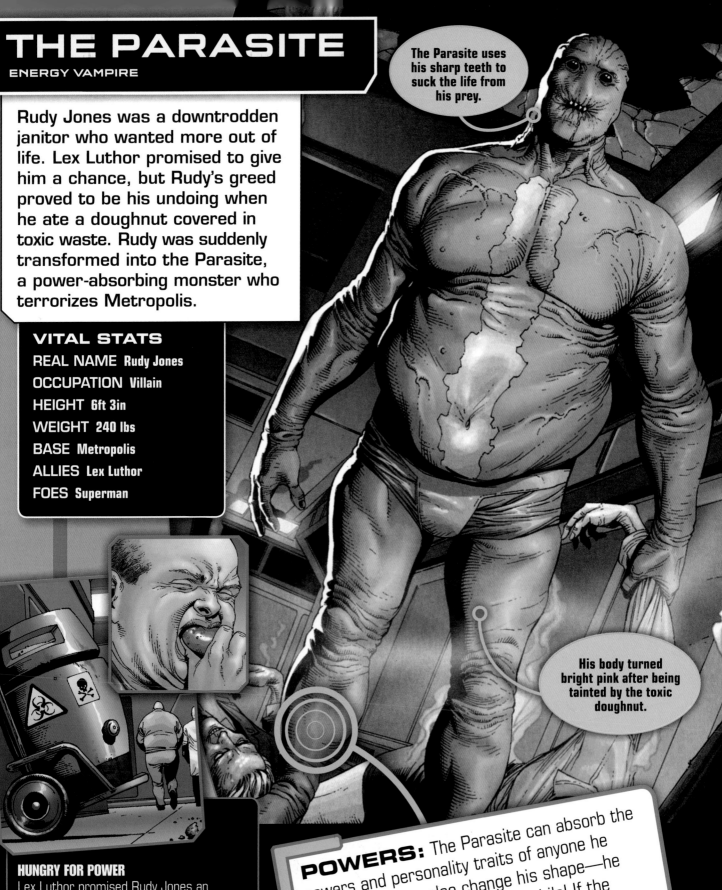

THE PARASITE
ENERGY VAMPIRE

Rudy Jones was a downtrodden janitor who wanted more out of life. Lex Luthor promised to give him a chance, but Rudy's greed proved to be his undoing when he ate a doughnut covered in toxic waste. Rudy was suddenly transformed into the Parasite, a power-absorbing monster who terrorizes Metropolis.

The Parasite uses his sharp teeth to suck the life from his prey.

VITAL STATS
REAL NAME Rudy Jones
OCCUPATION Villain
HEIGHT 6ft 3in
WEIGHT 240 lbs
BASE Metropolis
ALLIES Lex Luthor
FOES Superman

His body turned bright pink after being tainted by the toxic doughnut.

HUNGRY FOR POWER
Lex Luthor promised Rudy Jones an education and the chance to become a true success. It was a false promise, and anyway, Rudy was more interested in money. But that hunger for money was soon to be replaced by a hunger for power!

POWERS: The Parasite can absorb the powers and personality traits of anyone he touches. He can also change his shape—he even posed as Lois Lane for a while! If the Parasite drains someone's entire life essence, he will destroy them. He craves Superman's power, but often finds it difficult to control.

THE PENGUIN
AVIAN ADVERSARY

The Penguin's short stature adds to his bird-like appearance.

As a child, Oswald Cobblepot was teased about his bird-like features. He grew up angry and resentful toward the world. Now he is the Penguin, one of Gotham City's most powerful crime bosses, He laughs in the faces of those who have wronged him, while he sits high atop his vast criminal empire.

VITAL STATS
REAL NAME Oswald Chesterfield Cobblepot
OCCUPATION Criminal
HEIGHT 5ft 2in
WEIGHT 175 lbs
BASE Gotham City
ALLIES The Joker, Black Mask
FOES Batman, Robin

He dresses with style, believing that one should always look one's best.

DOUBLE-CROSSED BIRDS
The Penguin once tricked the Birds of Prey team into rescuing him from a staged assassination attempt. The Birds later discovered that the double-crossing Penguin was actually after top secret files on the super hero community.

POWERS: The Penguin has no powers and is not a smart fighter, but he is a master at manipulating his enemies into destroying one another. The Penguin relies on a variety of trick umbrellas that can shoot bullets and acid, among other things. He also takes pleasure in planning elaborate bird-themed crimes.

PHANTOM STRANGER
WANDERING SPIRIT

Not much is known about the mysterious Phantom Stranger. Some say he is a fallen angel, forced to wander the Earth and provide help to those in need. Though he has been offered membership in the Justice League many times, Phantom Stranger prefers to do his noble work his own way—alone.

VITAL STATS

REAL NAME Unknown

OCCUPATION Hero

HEIGHT 6ft 2in

WEIGHT 185 lbs

BASE Mobile

ALLIES Justice League of America, Superboy

FOES Spectre, Eclipso

He can see ghosts and spirits invisible to the human eye.

Phantom Stranger knows everything about the past, present, and future.

He uses a mystical talisman to tame his supernatural energies.

MAGIC MOUSE
When Earth was attacked by the Spectre, the planet's magical beings gathered to combat his evil forces. The Spectre feared the vast powers of the Phantom Stranger so much that he turned him into a mouse, warning other magic-wielders not to interfere.

POWERS: Phantom Stranger has mastered a variety of supernatural energies, but his true powers are shrouded in mystery and defy classification. He has been known to help heroes make certain choices, moving them through the moral dilemmas they face. He can also teleport from place to place.

Hartley Rathaway was born deaf. After many surgeries, however, he was cured—and discovered he was gifted with a keen ear for music. Bored with his mundane life, Hartley turned his music into a weapon, becoming the Pied Piper, a master thief and criminal. He later reformed and befriended the Flash.

VITAL STATS

REAL NAME Hartley Rathaway

OCCUPATION Hero (reformed villain)

HEIGHT 5ft 10in

WEIGHT 150 lbs

BASE Central City

ALLIES The Flash, Kid Flash

FOES The Rogues

Pied Piper's flute plays a deadly melody that controls the mind.

His sonic tuning fork can paralyze anyone within range of its sound.

POWERS: Pied Piper is a technological wizard and an expert at mixing science and sound. He uses his musical abilities to perfect his sonic creations. Piper's instruments can be used to create sonic waves that mesmerize and control people. Since his reformation, Piper prefers compassion to violence.

ROGUE RIVAL
Pied Piper was framed for his parents' murder by Mirror Master, his former teammate in the Rogues. Piper was sent to prison, but managed to break out and convince the Flash of his innocence. Eventually, all charges against him were dropped and it was revealed that Mirror Master himself was the true murderer.

PLASTIC MAN
RUBBER RAIDER

Eel O'Brian was just a lowlife gangster until he was bathed in experimental acids that altered his body—and his mind. Vowing to turn his life around and quit crime for good, Eel became the humorous and heroic Plastic Man. He's now a committed crime fighter and a valued member of the Justice League.

VITAL STATS

REAL NAME Patrick "Eel" O'Brian

OCCUPATION Hero

HEIGHT 6ft 1in

WEIGHT 175 lbs

BASE Mobile

ALLIES Justice League of America, Freedom Fighters

FOES Fernus, Rama Khan

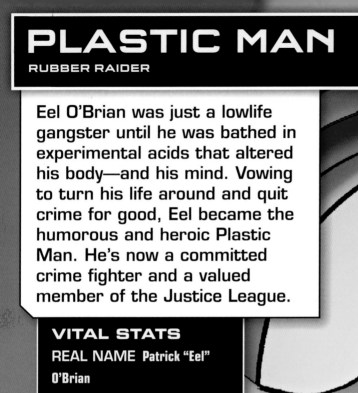

OFFSPRING

Plastic Man only recently found out that he has a son. The boy, called Offspring, has inherited all Plastic Man's stretchable powers and has even started a heroic career as a member of the Teen Titans. Plastic Man wishes he had a stronger relationship with Offspring and has vowed to be a

The chemicals that gave him his powers also keep him looking youthful.

Plastic Man is able to regenerate his body parts.

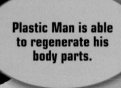

POWERS: Plastic Man is able to change his body and stretch into various shapes. His ability to alter his form makes him extremely agile and he is able to slip in and out of areas virtually unnoticed. Plastic Man has a weakness which can make his body

POISON IVY
PLANT PRINCESS

Pamela Isley was a shy doctor until the villainous Floronic Man used flower and plant toxins on her. They turned Pamela into a half-human, half-plant creature called Poison Ivy. The stunning but deadly Ivy now sees herself as Earth's protector. She often finds herself at odds with Batman, whom she tries to tempt with evil.

Her skin is green due to the deadly toxins that flow through her body.

Poison Ivy uses her vines to strangle her prey.

VITAL STATS
REAL NAME Doctor Pamela Lillian Isley
OCCUPATION Criminal
HEIGHT 5ft 6in
WEIGHT 135 lbs
BASE Gotham City
ALLIES Harley Quinn, Catwoman
FOES Batman, Robin

PLANT POWER
Poison Ivy lives in the abandoned Gotham City Animal Shelter with fellow villains Harley Quinn and Catwoman. The trio of criminals have found it easy to work together, but trouble seems to follow them, no matter where they go.

POWERS: As Doctor Isley, she was a gifted scientist with a vast knowledge of plant life. As Poison Ivy, she attacks those who threaten Earth's natural environment. Ivy is immune to most toxins and her "poison kiss" can paralyze her foes. She has control over plants and often uses fast-growing seed pods as weapons.

POWER GIRL

SUPER ALLY

Power Girl is from another universe. She came to our planet during an event known as the Crisis on Infinite Earths, when thousands of parallel worlds were destroyed. At first, Power Girl struggled with her identity, but Superman helped her to remember who she was and she now serves proudly with the Justice Society.

For years Power Girl suffered from amnesia and had no memory of her past.

VITAL STATS

REAL NAME Karen "Kara" Starr

OCCUPATION Hero

HEIGHT 5ft 7in

WEIGHT 160 lbs

BASE New York City

ALLIES Justice Society of America, Superman

FOES Ultra-Humanite, Superboy-Prime

Unlike most super heroes, she does not wear a symbol on her costume.

NIGHTWING OF KANDOR

When the villains Ultraman and Saturn Queen tried to take control of the bottled city of Kandor, Power Girl and Supergirl united against them. They went undercover as the Kryptonian heroes Nightwing and Flamebird to thwart the duo's evil plans.

POWERS: Earth's yellow sun grants Power Girl many different abilities such as super-strength, speed, and invulnerability. She also has heat vision and freezing breath. Power Girl is weakened by red sun energy as well as Kryptonite. Though she sometimes displays a fiery temper, her leadership skills are admired.

PROFESSOR HUGO STRANGE

CRIMINAL OF THE MIND

Despite being insane, Strange has a brilliantly deductive mind.

Professor Hugo Strange hates the idea of vigilante heroes and has developed a dangerous obsession with Batman. Having figured out the Dark Knight's secret identity, Strange spends much time trying to destroy Gotham City's masked protector.

VITAL STATS

REAL NAME Hugo Strange
OCCUPATION Psychiatrist, Criminal
HEIGHT 5ft 10in
WEIGHT 170 lbs
BASE Gotham City
ALLIES None
FOES Batman, Nightwing

BAT WANNABE

Hugo Strange harbors a secret desire to become Batman. Strange is so envious of the exciting life that he imagines Batman to have, that he often daydreams about fighting crime and protecting the city as the masked and caped crusader.

POWERS: Professor Hugo Strange is a master criminal strategist with an extensive knowledge of psychology. He's also developed many mind-altering drugs and chemicals, which he uses to control his victims. Strange is a strong hand-to-hand fighter, though he prefers to engage his opponents in mental combat.

PROMETHEUS
TECHNO-FIGHTER

After Prometheus saw the lives of his criminal parents violently taken by a police officer, he dedicated his life to destroying the forces of justice and peace. He trained his body and mind to the peak of human ability before chaneling his rage against the team that symbolized everything he hated—the Justice League.

His helmet is always updated with the latest technology.

VITAL STATS
REAL NAME Unknown
OCCUPATION Villain
HEIGHT 6ft 5in
WEIGHT 180 lbs
BASE Ghost Zone
ALLIES Lex Luthor, Injustice League
FOES Batman, Justice Leage of America

Prometheus uses a powerful, energy-charged nightstick in battle.

DEADLY DILEMMA
Prometheus was once captured by the JLA. However, he had already set a number of bombs to explode, and threatened to destroy their home cities unless they let him go. The JLA were forced to make the terrible decision to free their enemy.

POWERS: Prometheus has extensive knowledge of advanced technology. His helmet can mimic the abilities of any fighter imaginable, making him virtually unstoppable. Even without his helmet, he is a very skilled fighter. Over the years Prometheus's mind has fragmented, leaving him more dangerous than ever.

THE QUESTION
DISGUISED DETECTIVE

The Question's mask is made of Pseudoderm, a substance that looks exactly like skin.

Renee Montoya was a Gotham City police officer in desperate need of guidance. Detective Vic Sage—a.k.a. the super hero Question—took Renee under his wing and trained her to overcome her self-doubt. Renee eventually became the new Question, and focuses her energy on exposing evil conspiracies.

The Question often appears shrouded in smoke to frighten her enemies.

VITAL STATS
REAL NAME Renee Montoya
OCCUPATION Hero
HEIGHT 5ft 8in
WEIGHT 144 lbs
BASE Gotham City
ALLIES Batwoman, Huntress
FOES Vandal Savage, Religion of Crime

POWERS: The Question is a world-class detective and investigator who mastered her skills while serving with the Gotham City Police Department. In addition to her police training, she's proficient in a variety of martial arts. She is also very good at controlling her emotions and can withstand large amounts of physical pain.

PASSING THE TORCH
Vic Sage was dying and knew he had to find an able and willing successor to his heroic identity. He tracked down Renee Montoya, choosing her as the one who would carry on his legacy. Reluctantly, Renee agreed to the rigorous training and soon became the new Question.

RA'S AL GHUL
THE DEMON'S HEAD

Ra's al Ghul is a formidable warrior and one of Batman's fiercest foes. He is centuries old and has fought in many wars and conquered many lands. Now a brutal terrorist, Ra's seeks to destroy humanity so that he can rebuild it as he chooses. Luckily, Batman stands in the way of his deadly plans.

VITAL STATS
REAL NAME Unknown
OCCUPATION Terrorist
HEIGHT 6ft 3in
WEIGHT 160 lbs
BASE Mobile
ALLIES Talia al Ghul, League of Assassins
FOES Batman, Nightwing

Although he is hundreds of years old, he only has a small amount of gray hair.

Ra's al Ghul is a master of martial arts.

THE LAZARUS PITS
Lazarus Pits are filled with mystical natural chemicals and are found in secret locations across the Earth. The pits can be used to return life to the dead or dying, however those who have been revived are stricken with short-term madness.

POWERS: Ra's al Ghul is immortal thanks to the mystical chemicals found in the Lazarus Pits. If he does not immerse himself in the pits regularly, he will perish. Having fought in numerous wars over the centuries, Ra's has become an exceptional fighter, and is a master of many different fighting styles.

RAVEN
DAUGHTER OF DARKNESS

Raven's telekinesis allows her to move objects with her mind.

Raven is the daughter of the cruel demon Trigon. Although she struggles to keep the dark side of her personality in check, Raven chooses to fight against evil. Trigon has tried to control Raven many times in his quest for ultimate power, but he is often thwarted by her loyal friends, the Teen Titans.

VITAL STATS
REAL NAME Rachel Roth
OCCUPATION Hero
HEIGHT 5ft 8in
WEIGHT 135 lbs
BASE San Francisco
ALLIES Teen Titans, Beast Boy
FOES Trigon

Raven has the ability to teleport to any location.

POWERS: Raven has mastered a number of mystical arts and is familiar with many otherworldly realms. She is also a powerful empath: she can take on someone else's physical trauma as her own, healing them in the process. Unfortunately, this causes Raven great pain and suffering.

SOUL SUPERPOWER
Raven can unleash a powerful force from within her known as her "soul-self." This force, which takes the form of a giant raven, can teleport Raven to different dimensions or travel alone as a separate entity. The soul-self can also fight on Raven's behalf, by entering the mind of her opponent.

RED HOOD
ROBIN-GONE-WRONG

Jason Todd began his career as Batman's heroic apprentice, the second Robin, but after a series of terrible events, he now operates as the villainous Red Hood. The Red Hood blames Batman for the tragedies in his life, and he now wreaks havoc upon Gotham City as he seeks revenge against the Dark Knight.

The hood is actually a helmet that contains a computer.

VITAL STATS

REAL NAME Jason Todd
OCCUPATION Villain
HEIGHT 6ft
WEIGHT 190 lbs
BASE Gotham City
ALLIES Scarlett
FOES Batman, Nightwing

REBORN
As Robin, Jason Todd died in an explosion, leaving Batman devastated. Jason was thought to be dead for many years, but returned to life after a huge cosmic event altered reality. When Batman and Jason were reunited in Gotham City, the Dark Knight was shocked to learn that his former ally had turned to evil.

POWERS: Red Hood is a fierce hand-to-hand combatant who has mastered many different fighting techniques. He is also a skilled gymnast and acrobat. Red Hood is a devious manipulator who enjoys pitting his fellow villains against one another, especially if the end result is the destruction of Batman.

RED ROBIN

Young Tim Drake used his sharp detective skills to figure out Batman's secret identity. The Dark Knight saw promise in the boy and trained him to become the third Robin. Now, as Red Robin, the adult Tim is a hero in his own right, traveling the world and working with other heroes to fight crime.

A collapsible bo staff is hidden on his costume but is easily available in a fight.

VITAL STATS
REAL NAME Tim Drake
OCCUPATION Hero
HEIGHT 5ft 6in
WEIGHT 145 lbs
BASE Gotham City
ALLIES Batman, Nightwing, Batgirl
FOES Captain Boomerang, Red Hood

Red Robin's utility belt contains smoke bombs and communication devices.

POWERS: Red Robin is a world-class detective and strategist who often works with a network of heroes around the world to help solve crimes. He is also well-versed in a variety of martial arts. Red Robin is a computer genius and has recently discovered an evil computer network that he has tasked himself to destroy.

TITANS TOGETHER
Red Robin and Superboy became close pals when they were both members of the Teen Titans. Red Robin still visits Superboy in Smallville when he wants to get away. The pair have seen their share of Earth-shattering battles, but through it all, their friendship remains strong.

RED TORNADO
CRIMSON WHIRLWIND

The Red Tornado is an android who was created by the mad scientist T.O. Morrow as a weapon against the Justice League of America. But Tornado has a mind of his own, and he went against his programming. He befriended the Justice League and became a committed team member.

VITAL STATS

REAL NAME John Smith

OCCUPATION Hero

HEIGHT 6ft 1in

WEIGHT 325 lbs

BASE Mobile

ALLIES Justice League of America

FOES T.O. Morrow

FAMILY MAN
Despite being an android, Red Tornado has found love and acceptance with his wife, Kathy, and daughter, Traya. They cherish their time with Red Tornado, but worry when he is on JLA missions.

A button on Red Tornado's neck can disarm him should he lose control.

Red Tornado can produce winds of up to 350 mph.

POWERS: Red Tornado's android body houses a powerful elemental force which gives him the ability to create cyclones, fly, and shoot blasts of wind. His winds can also act as a force field and deflect attacks. Red Tornado's body has been rebuilt many times, growing stronger with each new upgrade.

THE RIDDLER
CAPTAIN OF CONUNDRUMS

The Riddler's insignia is a question mark.

Young Edward Nigma loved solving puzzles and stumping people with his riddles. As an adult, Edward turned to crime and became the Riddler, a master criminal who lives to torment the people of Gotham City. Though he's tried going straight, the Riddler is still at odds with Batman.

VITAL STATS

REAL NAME Edward Nigma
OCCUPATION Criminal
HEIGHT 6ft 1in
WEIGHT 185 lbs
BASE Gotham City
ALLIES Hush, Ra's al Ghul
FOES Batman, Robin

He carries a cane with a question mark-shaped handle.

POWERS: The Riddler is a brilliant criminal strategist, who loves watching his enemies struggle to solve his intricate riddles. He is an average hand-to-hand fighter, but often uses elaborate puzzle-themed weaponry and traps. He prefers to work alone, but has, at times, employed attractive female assistants.

JOINING FORCES
The Riddler sees himself as far superior to most of the other villains, and believes they lack true commitment. However, when he was approached by Poison Ivy, Catwoman, and Harley Quinn after they were framed for a murder, he agreed to help them solve the mystery.

ROBIN
THE BOY WONDER

Damian Wayne was raised by assassins and trained from an early age to be a cold-hearted fighter. But he eventually rejected evil and donned a hero's costume, becoming the newest Robin. Batman may find his new sidekick difficult to get along with, but Damian's passion is unmatched.

Robin can mimic the vocal patterns of anyone he hears.

His costume has an optional hood for extra secrecy.

Robin's utility belt contains tracers, first aid kits, and communication devices.

VITAL STATS

REAL NAME Damian Wayne
OCCUPATION Hero
HEIGHT 5ft 2in
WEIGHT 120 lbs
BASE Gotham City
ALLIES Batman, Teen Titans
FOES Ra's al Ghul

TROUBLESOME TITAN
Young Robin can be very forceful and is sometimes overconfident. In an effort to help himself adjust to a heroic life, Robin briefly joined the Teen Titans. The team tried their best to help Robin control his short temper, but the young hero saw himself as a superior team leader and wasn't afraid to say so.

POWERS: Robin has mastered a variety of martial arts despite his young age. He is an expert in hand-to-hand combat, and is very agile due to his small size. Robin's detective skills are strong, and he continues to learn additional skills and disciplines every day, although he can be incredibly impatient at times.

ROCKET RED
RUSSIAN RAMPART

Gavril Ivanovich once led an elite Russian army force known as the Rocket Red Brigade. Following a disagreement with his teammates, he left—and became the armored hero Rocket Red. Recently, he's teamed up with members of the Justice League to help track down the evil businessman, Maxwell Lord.

The design of Rocket Red's armor is based on the Russian flag.

This armor was created by Green Lantern trainer Kilowog.

VITAL STATS

REAL NAME Gavril Ivanovich
OCCUPATION Hero
HEIGHT 6ft 2in
WEIGHT 325 lbs
BASE Russia
ALLIES Justice League of America
FOES Maxwell Lord

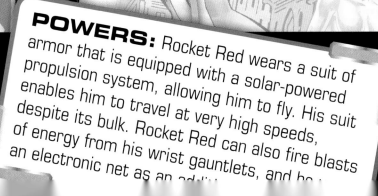

ROCKET RED BRIGADE

Gavril Ivanovich was a committed member of the Rocket Red Brigade, but despised his teammates' approach to politics. He stuck to his beliefs and came to blows with his squadron. Thankfully, the Justice League of America welcomed him to their team.

POWERS: Rocket Red wears a suit of armor that is equipped with a solar-powered propulsion system, allowing him to fly. His suit enables him to travel at very high speeds, despite its bulk. Rocket Red can also fire blasts of energy from his wrist gauntlets, and he
an electronic net as an add...

SANDMAN
SILICON SLEUTH

Sandy Hawkins grew up fighting crime as a member of the heroic All-Star Squadron. Then a horrible accident transformed him into a creature made entirely of sand. After learning how to control his new powers, Sandy continued his war against crime—alongside the JSA—as the prophetic hero, Sandman.

VITAL STATS

REAL NAME Sanderson "Sandy" Hawkins

OCCUPATION Hero

HEIGHT 5ft 11in

WEIGHT 162 lbs

BASE New York City

ALLIES Justice Society of America

FOES Mordru, Geomancer

Sandman wears a frightening gas mask to strike fear in the hearts of criminals.

Sandman uses sleeping gas to knock his enemies out.

SAND MONSTER
When an experimental gun exploded, Sandy was showered in radioactive silica particles that turned him into a raging sand monster. Sandy's mentor placed him in suspended animation until he found a cure—a cure that left Sandy able to transform into sand at will!

POWERS: Sandman's body is made of a substance that enables him to manipulate anything containing sand. He can become as hard as rock or disperse himself into the Earth. Sandman is also a trained detective. He has recently discovered that his dreams are really visions of the future.

SATURN GIRL
MIND MAIDEN

Saturn Girl's mental powers are capable of casting illusions.

Saturn Girl was born in the 31st century on Titan, the largest of Saturn's moons. She was one of the founding members of the Legion of Super-Heroes, and is very passionate about her team. Using her telepathic powers, she can often sense looming danger, and does not hesitate to risk her life for her colleagues.

VITAL STATS
REAL NAME Imra Ardeen
OCCUPATION Legionnaire
HEIGHT 5ft 7in
WEIGHT 120 lbs
BASE 31st century Earth
ALLIES Legion of Super-Heroes
FOES Legion of Super-Villains

Saturn Girl sometimes flies using her flight belt, rather than her Legion flight ring.

POWERS: Saturn Girl is considered a 10th level telepath which makes her extremely powerful. She can read people's minds and link with a team as large as the Legion. Saturn Girl can also project bolts of energy from her mind which she can use to stun her opponents.

SUPERMOM
Saturn Girl's home world of Titan was recently destroyed, and her twin sons, Grahm and Garridan, kidnapped. Fortunately, Saturn Girl was able to recover them with the help of her husband, Lightning Lad. After this awful experience, the couple decided to take a leave of absence from the Legion to spend some time together as a family.

SCARECROW
PROFESSOR OF FRIGHT

The Scarecrow was once a professor at Gotham University called Doctor Jonathan Crane. When his colleagues deemed his experiments too dangerous, Crane became the Scarecrow and sought revenge on them. Now only Batman stands in his way as he tries to spread chaos and fear through Gotham City.

VITAL STATS
REAL NAME Doctor Jonathan Crane
OCCUPATION Villain
HEIGHT 6ft
WEIGHT 120 lbs
BASE Gotham City
ALLIES Secret Society of Super-Villains, Sinestro Corps
FOES Batman, Robin

Though scary in appearance, Scarecrow himself is not very brave.

He releases his fear gas through interconnected tubes in his costume.

CHILDHOOD TROUBLES
As a boy, Jonathan Crane was relentlessly teased by his classmates for being obsessed with his studies. After being embarrassed at his high school prom, Crane donned his frightening Scarecrow costume for the first time—and learned how addictive spreading fear could be.

POWERS: The Scarecrow is a trained chemist who mixes a variety of compounds to make his dangerous fear toxins. These toxins can make people hallucinate, bringing their worst fears to life. The Scarecrow is also a master of psychological warfare and enjoys watching his victims squirm as he tortures them.

SECRET SIX
CAGEY CRIMINALS

The Secret Six is a group of tough, unpredictable criminals. They were brought together by a mysterious figure called Mockingbird. But the team defied Mockingbird's orders and ventured out on its own. The Secret Six is motivated by money and will take any job if the price is right.

MEMBERS INCLUDE

1 BANE The brutish Bane sees himself as Scandal's protector, though she dismisses his advances.

2 DEADSHOT Deadshot claims that he never misses a target. The mercenary stays with the group strictly for the money.

3 JEANETTE Jeanette is an immortal Banshee whose piercing scream has a devastating effect on all who hear it.

4 CATMAN Catman has a keen sense of smell, and discovered his incredible tracking ability while living with a pride of lions.

5 RAGDOLL The mentally unstable Ragdoll can twist his body into a variety of shapes.

6 SCANDAL As the daughter of Vandal Savage, Scandal shares her father's vicious streak.

HELL CARD
The Secret Six were once sent on a wild chase looking for a mysterious card that contained the words, "Get Out Of Hell Free." They realized that the card would allow them to escape from Hell, should they ever end up there—which seemed quite likely!

SERGEANT ROCK
BATTLING BRIGADIER

Sergeant Rock fought during World War II and is a respected and highly decorated soldier. He was the leader of Easy Company, a group of diverse commandos who served in every major war. Later in life, Rock worked with Amanda Waller and her Suicide Squad, where his battle experience came in handy.

VITAL STATS

REAL NAME Frank Rock
OCCUPATION Hero
HEIGHT 6ft
WEIGHT 183 lbs
BASE Mobile
ALLIES Easy Company
FOES Axis Powers

Sergeant Rock's dog tags have sentimental value.

Rock equips himself with guns and grenades for defense.

WAR HERO
Sergeant Rock has seen triumph and tragedy on the battlefield and remains a committed leader to those that serve with him. Rock often feels burdened by his role as leader, but war is not without sacrifice—and no one knows that better than him.

POWERS: Sergeant Rock is an expertly trained fighter and marksman. He is a keen tactician and planner, having led many battalions of soldiers through the years. He also has extensive knowledge of weaponry. Though he doesn't have any superpowers, Sergeant Rock always keeps his body in peak physical condition.

Her ghoulish appearance makes her a frightening foe.

SILVER BANSHEE
SINFUL SIREN

Siobhan McDougal is cursed with the ghastly powers of the Silver Banshee. To free herself from the curse, she must locate her family's ancient artifacts. The search has taken Banshee to Metropolis, where her willingness to destroy anyone who stood in her way led to a confrontation with Supergirl.

Silver Banshee can also use her sonic abilities to teleport.

VITAL STATS
REAL NAME Siobhan McDougal
OCCUPATION Villain
HEIGHT 6ft
WEIGHT 160 lbs
BASE Mobile
ALLIES Secret Society of Super-Villains
FOES Supergirl, Superman

POWERS: Silver Banshee's voice can produce a deafening, high-pitched sound known as a death wail. This power can disorient her opponents—even drive them out of their mind. It is believed that the Silver Banshee can destroy someone by speaking their true name. She also possesses superhuman strength and speed.

CRY OF THE BANSHEE
On her quest to secure her family's treasures, Banshee once found herself face to face with Supergirl in Metropolis. Using her death wail, she turned Supergirl into a horrifying Banshee hybrid. But with the help of Inspector Henderson, Supergirl was later cured.

SINESTRO
FEAR-MONGER

Sinestro was once a heroic Green Lantern, but was stripped of his ring after the Guardians discovered he was using his powers to rule his home planet, Korugar. Banished to the anti-matter world of Qward, he found a yellow power ring and now spreads fear across the galaxy as leader of his own evil Sinestro Corps.

VITAL STATS

REAL NAME Thal Sinestro
OCCUPATION Villain
HEIGHT 6ft 7in
WEIGHT 205 lbs
BASE Qward
ALLIES Parallax, Sinestro Corps
FOES Green Lantern, Mongul

The color of Sinestro's uniform represents his yellow, fear-based energy powers.

WAR OF THE LANTERNS
Sinestro strongly objected to Hal Jordan inheriting Abin Sur's Green Lantern ring, believing that Hal would dishonor the Corps with his foolish bravado. But in the end, it was Sinestro who soiled the Corps' reputation, when he turned toward a life of evil.

POWERS: Sinestro's yellow power ring is fueled by the power of fear and can create hard-light energy constructs similar to those of a Green Lantern. Sinestro has mastered the use of his power ring, but he's also a well-trained hand-to-hand combatant. He enjoys inflicting as much pain on his opponents as possible.

SOLOMON GRUNDY
SINISTER SWAMPMAN

Solomon Grundy was once an evil merchant named Cyrus Gold. When Gold's murdered body was thrown into Slaughter Swamp, supernatural forces turned him into a zombie-like creature. Now as the brutish Solomon Grundy, he has turned to a life of crime, but often ends up being used by those smarter than him.

VITAL STATS

REAL NAME Cyrus Gold
OCCUPATION Villain
HEIGHT 7ft 5in
WEIGHT 517 lbs
BASE Mobile
ALLIES Injustice Society
FOES Justice Society of America

Grundy has pale gray skin and smells like swamp water.

POWERS: Solomon Grundy has super-human strength, stamina, and invulnerability. He's also been granted immortality through the mystical energies of Slaughter Swamp. Whenever his body is destroyed, Grundy's massive brute form is able to rise from the dead, though he often returns with varying levels of intelligence.

SMART SOLOMON
After being reborn with a high level of intelligence, Grundy enlisted Professor Ivo to help him steal Red Tornado's body and turn it into a form in which he could live forever. When the JLA foiled Grundy's plans, he demolished them. Little did he know they would return to destroy him.

SPECTRE
SPIRIT OF VENGEANCE

Gotham City detective Crispus Allen lost his life in the line of duty. His body, however, was soon inhabited by the otherworldly Spectre, giving him a second chance to defend the innocent. Now as the spirit of vengeance, the Spectre seeks justice for those who have been wronged.

VITAL STATS

REAL NAME Crispus Allen
OCCUPATION Conflicted Hero
HEIGHT 6ft
WEIGHT 180 lbs
BASE Mobile
ALLIES Justice Society of America
FOES Eclipso

He is still recognizable as Crispus Allen—but in a much ghostlier form.

The Spectre can grow his ghostly body to giant size.

SPECTRAL PROTECTOR

After Crispus Allen became possessed by the Spectre, he was no longer able to communicate with his friends and family. However, despite feelings of loneliness, Allen found he could still protect his loved ones in his new, shadowy identity as the ghostly avenger.

POWERS: The Spectre is one of the most powerful forces in the universe and has total cosmic awareness of all things. He is able to change the shape and size of his body and can teleport anywhere he chooses. The Spectre can also fly and become invisible, although the full extent of his powers remains a mystery.

SPEEDY
ACE ARCHER

Mia Dearden was a runaway from an abusive home who was taken in by the hero Green Arrow. Keen to fight alongside the Emerald Archer, Mia began training hard, despite his objections that it was too risky. Mia persisted, and finally became the second hero to serve as his daring sidekick, Speedy.

Speedy often uses trick arrows given to her by Green Arrow.

VITAL STATS

REAL NAME Mia Dearden
OCCUPATION Hero
HEIGHT 5ft 4in
WEIGHT 105 lbs
BASE Star City
ALLIES Green Arrow, Teen Titans
FOES Electrocutioner, Doctor Light

POWERS: Speedy was trained as a street fighter but has since learned many different martial arts. She's also a gifted acrobat, a proficient archer, and quite agile in battle. Though she is still young, Speedy has a passion for excellence and constantly impresses Green Arrow with her skills.

SIDEKICK
Speedy has become an important member of Green Arrow's extended family since she arrived in Star City. Through study and training, Speedy has learned a lot from her mentor's years of experience. However, she has also taught him a thing or two in the process!

STARFIRE
WARRIOR PRINCESS

Starfire was a princess on the planet Tamaran. Although she was trained as a warrior from childhood, she lived a relatively carefree life until the day her people were enslaved. After fleeing to nearby Earth, Starfire joined the Teen Titans super hero team, who helped her overthrow her planet's captors.

VITAL STATS
REAL NAME Koriand'r
OCCUPATION Hero
HEIGHT 6ft 4in
WEIGHT 158 lbs
BASE Tamaran
ALLIES Donna Troy, Teen Titans
FOES Blackfire, Lady Styx

Her body can absorb ultraviolet radiation and use it to fly.

Starfire possesses superhuman strength.

BLACKFIRE
Blackfire is Starfire's jealous older sister. She cannot harness solar power and blames Starfire for taking what she believes is rightfully hers. In her endless quest for dominance and revenge, Blackfire has aligned herself with some of the universe's most despicable villains.

MICHAEL TURNER

POWERS: Starfire can absorb solar power and use it to project powerful bursts of energy known as starbolts. She is trained in martial arts and many alien fighting styles. She can also fly and withstand the harshness of space travel. Though Starfire has a feisty temper, her presence often has a calming effect.

STARGIRL
YOUNG CRUSADER

Stargirl's Cosmic Staff can produce force fields and energy blasts.

Young Courtney Whitmore found her stepfather's Cosmic Converter Belt and discovered he was once a super hero called the Star-Spangled Kid. Courtney realized she was destined to be a hero, too, and became the strong-willed Stargirl. She now serves proudly with the Justice Society of America.

VITAL STATS
REAL NAME Courtney Whitmore
OCCUPATION Hero
HEIGHT 5ft 5in
WEIGHT 127 lbs
BASE Blue Valley, Nebraska
ALLIES Justice Society of America
FOES Per Degaton, Shiv

The Cosmic Converter Belt projects tiny shooting stars that confuse her foes.

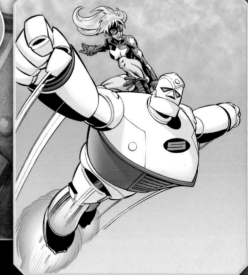

POWERS: Stargirl inherited her Cosmic Staff from the hero Starman when he retired. Using the staff and her Cosmic Converter Belt, she is able to fly and harness stellar energy. Stargirl is also a trained gymnast and acrobat. She has studied hand-to-hand combat with her Justice Society teammates.

STAR AND S.T.R.I.P.E.
Stargirl's stepfather, Pat Dugan, was worried that Stargirl might find herself in trouble. He created a robotic suit of battle armor called S.T.R.I.P.E. (Special Tactics Robotic Integrated Power Enhancer), and began to escort her everywhere. Stargirl was embarrassed, but understood that he was only trying to help.

STARMAN
GALACTIC GUARDIAN

Starman is a time traveler from the future, and a member of the Legion of Super-Heroes. His adventures have taken him across many different universes, and bouncing around the cosmos has made him mentally unpredictable. But Starman always follows his heart back to the future and into the arms of Dream Girl.

VITAL STATS
REAL NAME Thom Kallor
OCCUPATION Legionnaire
HEIGHT 5ft 8in
WEIGHT 160 lbs
BASE 21st century Earth
ALLIES Legion of Super-Heroes, Justice Society of America
FOES Kenz Nuhor, Gog

Starman possesses super-strength, speed, and durability.

His costume is a map of different universes and was created by Brainiac 5.

DREAM GIRL
Dream Girl (a.k.a. Nura Nal) is Starman's 31st century girlfriend and Legion teammate. Nura's power to see the future recently drew the attention of the evil Doctor Destiny, who kidnapped her and transported her to the 21st century. But Starman and the rest of the Legion of Super-Heroes were quick to travel back in time to save her.

POWERS: Starman has the power to make any object he chooses extremely heavy—even himself! However, he must be very careful when using his power in case he accidentally creates a deadly black hole which could destroy the universe. Starman can also travel between universes, using his costume as a map.

STARRO
STARFISH CONQUEROR

Starro the Conqueror is a giant creature shaped like a starfish who wanders the universe in search of planets to enslave. To conquer a planet, he sends out millions of smaller versions of himself to possess its citizens. Starro often targets Earth, but is always defeated by the Justice League of America.

VITAL STATS

REAL NAME Inapplicable
OCCUPATION Conqueror
HEIGHT Inapplicable
WEIGHT Inapplicable
BASE Mobile
ALLIES None
FOES Justice League of America

Starro's alien body is invulnerable to most physical attacks.

He can produce powerful energy blasts from his tentacles.

Starro sends out smaller drones to scout locations to conquer.

ALIEN ATTACK

Starro once attacked New York City and took control of the Justice League in the process. As an android, Red Tornado's mind was immune to Starro's control and he used this advantage to defeat the alien starfish. Together, Tornado and the revived JLA used freezing ice to thwart Starro's attempt at total domination.

POWERS: Starro can control a person's mind by attaching himself to their face, putting his victims into a dream-like trance. He can also possess their body and force them to battle. He has super-strength and can be very difficult to remove once attached. Starro is also able to reproduce at an extremely high rate.

STAR SAPPHIRE
VIOLET VICTOR

Carol Ferris was in charge of an airline. Then an alien race of women from the planet Zamaron granted her the abilities of the Star Sapphire, and a power ring fueled by the emotion of love. Originally an enemy of Green Lantern Hal Jordan, this reluctant hero has now become Hal's loyal ally.

> She must charge her power ring with a Star Sapphire power battery.

> The Star Sapphire gem can project violet force fields.

VITAL STATS

REAL NAME Carol Ferris
OCCUPATION Hero
HEIGHT 5ft 7in
WEIGHT 125 lbs
BASE Coast City
ALLIES Green Lantern
FOES Sinestro

LEADING LADY
Carol Ferris became the head of Ferris Aircraft when her father, the company's owner, became ill. Strong-willed Carol often clashed with employee—and boyfriend—Hal Jordan, also known as Green Lantern, while trying to keep the company from going bankrupt during her father's absence.

POWERS: Star Sapphire possesses the mysterious Star Sapphire gem which influences those around her with feelings of warmth and love. Her violet power ring grants her above-average strength and speed, and its energy enables her to fly, travel in space, and create energy constructs (solid forms).

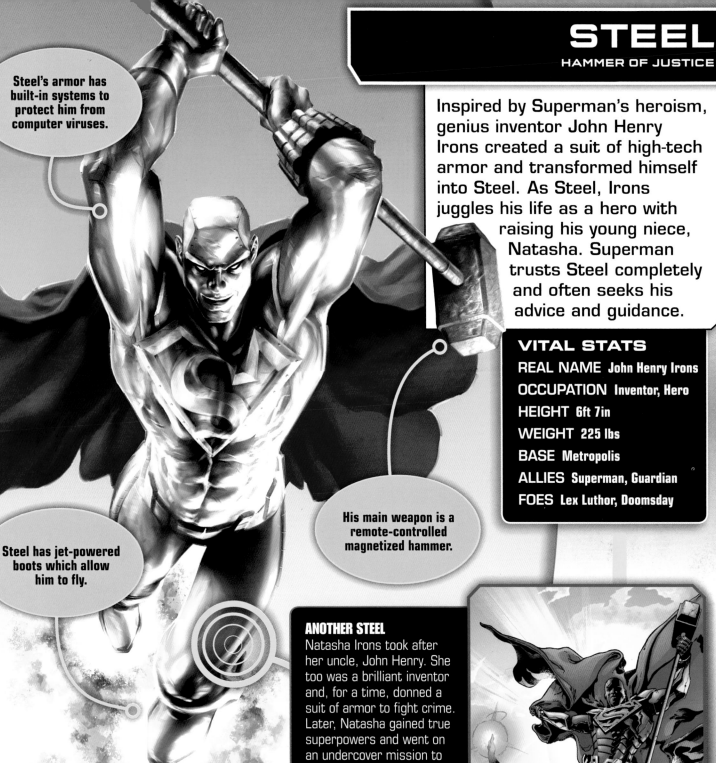

STEEL
HAMMER OF JUSTICE

Steel's armor has built-in systems to protect him from computer viruses.

Inspired by Superman's heroism, genius inventor John Henry Irons created a suit of high-tech armor and transformed himself into Steel. As Steel, Irons juggles his life as a hero with raising his young niece, Natasha. Superman trusts Steel completely and often seeks his advice and guidance.

VITAL STATS
REAL NAME John Henry Irons
OCCUPATION Inventor, Hero
HEIGHT 6ft 7in
WEIGHT 225 lbs
BASE Metropolis
ALLIES Superman, Guardian
FOES Lex Luthor, Doomsday

His main weapon is a remote-controlled magnetized hammer.

Steel has jet-powered boots which allow him to fly.

ANOTHER STEEL
Natasha Irons took after her uncle, John Henry. She too was a brilliant inventor and, for a time, donned a suit of armor to fight crime. Later, Natasha gained true superpowers and went on an undercover mission to spy on a super-team created by Lex Luthor.

POWERS: Steel has a genius-level intellect and an extremely creative mind, with which he created his sleek, stylized armor. He operates out of his Steelworks facility in Metropolis where he's constantly inventing new technology. Steel's bravery in the face of danger is one of his most admired attribu...

SUICIDE SQUAD
TASK FORCE X

Task Force X—known as the Suicide Squad to its members—is a team of ruthless superhuman criminals. They take on covert missions too dangerous for an ordinary team, with the promise of freedom if they succeed. Directed by Amanda Waller, this fearless team will get any job done.

MEMBERS INCLUDE

1 CHEMO Chemo bathes his foes in a chemical cocktail.

2 NIGHTSHADE Nightshade sends her enemies to dark dimensions.

3 CARAPAX Carapax wears an experimental high-tech suit of armor.

4 WINDFALL Windfall is able to create weapons out of thin air.

5 DEADSHOT Deadshot is an expert marksman and Waller's longtime ally.

6 CAPTAIN BOOMERANG JR. Owen Mercer has super-speed and uses deadly trick boomerangs.

7 PLASTIQUE Plastique is a deadly explosives expert.

8 RICK FLAG Rick Flag is the team's trusted field commander.

9 COUNT VERTIGO Count Vertigo uses magnetic power to disorient foes.

10 BRONZE TIGER Bronze Tiger is a martial arts master.

11 WHITE DRAGON William Heller believes in inequality for all.

FACE OFF
Amanda Waller has been known to hold cruel grudges against friend and foe alike. In her early days she often worked with military man Wade Eiling, who has since become the monstrous General. Recently, she did not hesitate in blackmailing him into working for her.

SUPERBOY
BOY OF STEEL

Superboy was created when scientists combined the DNA of both Superman and Lex Luthor to form a copy of the Man of Steel. Mixed-up Superboy struggled to find peace within himself, but at last felt complete when he joined the fight for justice alongside his heroic friends in the Teen Titans.

Superboy recently discovered that he has x-ray vision.

Superboy lifts objects not with strength, but with a mental power called tactile telekinesis.

VITAL STATS
REAL NAME Kon-El/Conner Kent
OCCUPATION Hero
HEIGHT 5ft 7in
WEIGHT 150 lbs
BASE Smallville
ALLIES Red Robin, Teen Titans
FOES Lex Luthor, Superboy-Prime

CADMUS CLONE
Superboy was born in the high-tech laboratory called Project Cadmus, where he was kept alive in a cloning tube. When Superman fell in battle against the deadly Doomsday, Superboy broke free of Cadmus's control and took to the skies as the newest hero of Metropolis.

POWERS: Superboy uses tactile telekinesis (special psychic energy) to mimic powers such as super-strength, flight, and invulnerability. He can also lift and tear things apart simply by touching them. Superboy's powers continue to develop: He recently discovered he has heat vision and freezing breath.

SUPERBOY-PRIME
MENACE OF STEEL

Superboy-Prime is a powerful teenager from a parallel world in which there were no heroes to inspire him. When he came to our planet, he became angry because he felt he had been rejected by Superman. The insecure teen has vowed to destroy the Man of Steel—and will obliterate anyone in his way.

VITAL STATS

REAL NAME Clark Kent
OCCUPATION Villain
HEIGHT 5ft 11in
WEIGHT 163 lbs
BASE Multiverse
ALLIES Sinestro, Cyborg Superman
FOES Superman, Superboy

Superboy-Prime's protective armor is modeled after the Anti-Monitor.

Unlike Superman, Superboy-Prime's body is not affected by magic.

BATTLE OF THE SUPERBOYS

In an effort to return to his home universe, Superboy-Prime worked together with a Lex Luthor from another world and attacked the heroes of our Earth. The misguided teen was eventually stopped by Superboy, who was badly injured during their battle.

POWERS: Superboy-Prime possesses super-strength, flight, and invulnerability. He has heightened senses as well as heat vision, x-ray vision, and freezing breath. He also wears a suit of armor that he uses to absorb energy. Though he was once innocent, Superboy-Prime's mind has lately become increasingly unstable.

Supergirl wears the same "S" symbol as her cousin Superman.

When the planet Krypton exploded, teenager Kara Zor-El was sent by rocketship to find her cousin Kal-El. Arriving on Earth years later, she found out that her cousin was the famous hero known as Superman. Kara decided to don her own blue and red costume and join her cousin's tireless crusade for justice as Supergirl.

VITAL STATS
REAL NAME Kara Zor-El/ Linda Lang
OCCUPATION Hero
HEIGHT 5ft 5in
WEIGHT 135 lbs
BASE Metropolis
ALLIES Superman, Lana Lang
FOES Silver Banshee, Darkseid

Supergirl is proficient in hand-to-hand combat from training with the Amazons.

PAWN OF DARKSEID
Shortly after her arrival on Earth, Supergirl was abducted by the tyrant Darkseid and brainwashed into becoming his evil slave. Thankfully, Superman and Batman were able to infiltrate Darkseid's citadel on the planet Apokolips and free Supergirl from the villain's mind control.

POWERS: Supergirl gains her powers from the light of Earth's yellow sun. They include heightened senses, super-strength, x-ray vision, heat vision, freezing breath, flight, and invulnerability. After arriving on Earth, she also trained with Wonder Woman and the Amazons on the island of Themyscira.

SUPERMAN
MAN OF STEEL

When the planet Krypton was destroyed, a baby called Kal-El was rocketed to Earth. He was raised in Smallville as Clark Kent until he discovered his immense powers. Clark has fulfilled his destiny by becoming Superman, legendary defender of Metropolis, where he uses his powers to fight relentlessly for justice.

VITAL STATS

REAL NAME Kal-El/Clark Kent
OCCUPATION Reporter, Hero
HEIGHT 6ft 3in
WEIGHT 235 lbs
BASE Metropolis
ALLIES Supergirl, Justice League of America
FOES Lex Luthor, Brainiac

The "S" symbol is actually his Kryptonian family crest.

Superman's body is vulnerable to Kryptonite and magic.

MEET CLARK KENT
Upon arriving in Metropolis, Superman found friendship with the staff of the *Daily Planet* newspaper. In order to protect his secret identity as Clark Kent, Superman wore glasses, changed his posture, and spoke differently, which was enough to fool those around him.

POWERS: The light of Earth's yellow sun grants Superman many different powers including invulnerability, super-strength, super-speed, and flight. Superman also has heightened senses as well as heat vision, x-ray vision, and freezing breath. As Clark Kent, he has a writer's instinct and a keen eye for storytelling.

Talia often turns her keen business mind to plotting complex schemes.

TALIA AL GHUL
DAUGHTER OF THE DEMON

For years, Talia al Ghul was manipulated and controlled by her villainous father, Ra's al Ghul. He convinced his daughter to help him destroy Batman. But Talia's rebellious streak finally emerged and she defied her father. Now, despite her devilish nature, Talia straddles the line between friend and foe of Batman.

She uses a variety of high-tech gear in her villainous life.

VITAL STATS
REAL NAME Talia al Ghul
OCCUPATION Villain
HEIGHT 5ft 8in
WEIGHT 140 lbs
BASE Mobile
ALLIES Ra's al Ghul, Injustice Society
FOES Batman, Robin

POWERS: Talia is immortal, but she must frequently rejuvenate herself in one of the life-giving Lazarus Pits. She's a martial arts master, a dangerous hand-to-hand combatant, and a skilled assassin. Talia is highly intelligent and capable of directing others. For a time, worked as the head of Lex

SECRET LOVE
Since she first laid eyes on Batman, Talia has been enamored of the Dark Knight and his skills as a fighter and detective. Talia's jealousy for Batman's affection often drives her to try and destroy him, but she secretly hopes that one day they will be together.

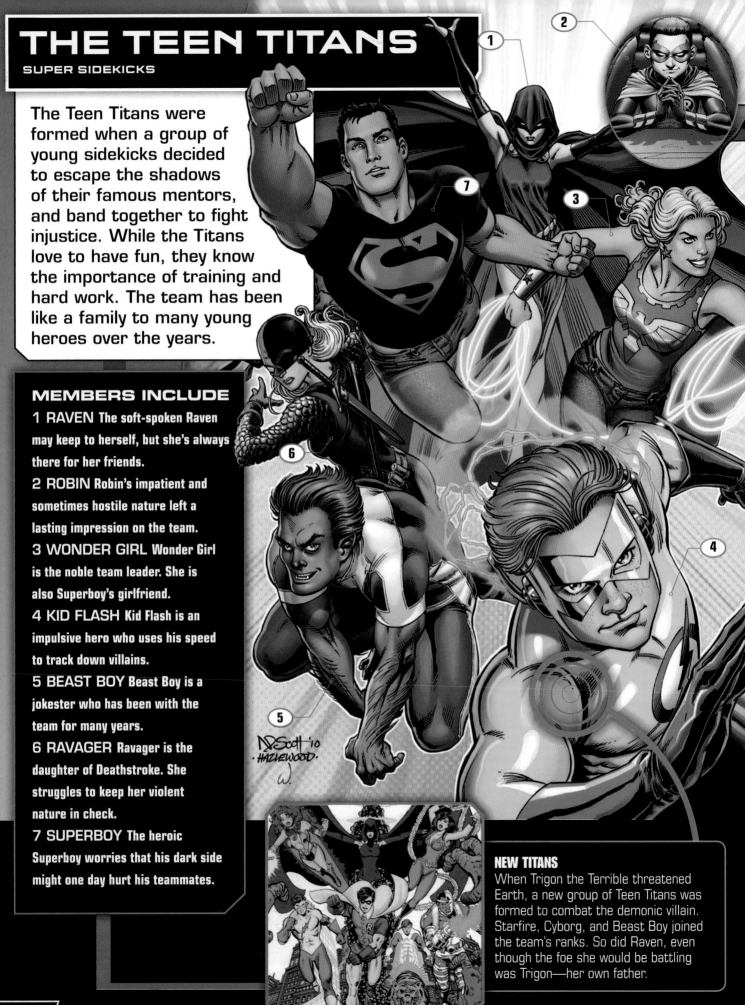

THE TEEN TITANS
SUPER SIDEKICKS

The Teen Titans were formed when a group of young sidekicks decided to escape the shadows of their famous mentors, and band together to fight injustice. While the Titans love to have fun, they know the importance of training and hard work. The team has been like a family to many young heroes over the years.

MEMBERS INCLUDE

1 RAVEN The soft-spoken Raven may keep to herself, but she's always there for her friends.

2 ROBIN Robin's impatient and sometimes hostile nature left a lasting impression on the team.

3 WONDER GIRL Wonder Girl is the noble team leader. She is also Superboy's girlfriend.

4 KID FLASH Kid Flash is an impulsive hero who uses his speed to track down villains.

5 BEAST BOY Beast Boy is a jokester who has been with the team for many years.

6 RAVAGER Ravager is the daughter of Deathstroke. She struggles to keep her violent nature in check.

7 SUPERBOY The heroic Superboy worries that his dark side might one day hurt his teammates.

NEW TITANS
When Trigon the Terrible threatened Earth, a new group of Teen Titans was formed to combat the demonic villain. Starfire, Cyborg, and Beast Boy joined the team's ranks. So did Raven, even though the foe she would be battling was Trigon—her own father.

TEMPEST
MYSTICAL MASTER

Garth's purple eyes made him an outcast in Atlantis.

As the original Aqualad, shy Garth was once Aquaman's apprentice and a member of the Teen Titans. He decided to further his studies by traveling to a secret realm and learning about the mystic arts from an ancient wizard. Now calling himself Tempest, Garth helps to protect the oceans from harm.

VITAL STATS
REAL NAME Garth
OCCUPATION Hero
HEIGHT 5ft 10in
WEIGHT 200 lbs
BASE Atlantis
ALLIES Aquaman, Mera
FOES Black Manta, Imperiex

Tempest can breathe underwater and communicate with marine creatures.

POWERS: Tempest has super-strength, stamina, and speed. He is also able to withstand deep ocean pressures. Tempest can sense the presence of magic in all things and is able to shoot blasts of powerful purple energy from his eyes. He can also manipulate water currents and boil or freeze liquids.

AQUALAD
Ancient Atlantean prophecy foretold that the young man known as Garth must be destroyed to protect the underwater kingdom. Thankfully, Aquaman chose to ingnore this warning. Instead, he saved Garth's life and trained him as his superpowered sidekick, Aqualad.

TERRA
EARTH-POWERED ANGEL

Terra is an alien who comes from deep beneath the Earth's crust. She was sent to the surface world to help protect the planet from those who seek to pollute and destroy it. Although she views humans as curious creatures, the optimistic Terra has struck up a friendship with fellow hero, Power Girl.

VITAL STATS
REAL NAME Atlee
OCCUPATION Hero
HEIGHT 5ft 5in
WEIGHT 125 lbs
BASE New York City
ALLIES Power Girl
FOES Ultra-Humanite, Deadcoil

She can shift tectonic plates with her mind, causing earthquakes and volcanic eruptions.

Terra can use even small shards of rock as projectile weapons.

POWER PALS
Since arriving on the surface world, Terra has befriended Power Girl, whom she considers a mentor and close friend. Recently, Terra was possessed by the evil Ultra-Humanite and it was up to Power Girl to save Terra's life—by taking on her own friend in battle.

POWERS: Terra possesses geokinesis, which is the ability to manipulate rock. She uses this power to turn pieces of the Earth into weapons. Terra is keenly attuned to the planet, and though her abilities are growing quickly, she is reluctant to fully embrace them, fearing the damage she might cause in the process.

TOMCAT

WILD WERE-CAT

As Tomcat, Tommy has sleek black fur and panther-like features.

Despite growing up with superpowers, Tommy Bronson never wanted the life of a hero. But everything changed when he discovered that his father was the legendary hero Wildcat. After being drafted into the Justice Society of America, Tommy began training as a true hero, taking the name Tomcat.

VITAL STATS

REAL NAME Thomas "Tommy" Bronson

OCCUPATION Hero

HEIGHT 5ft 6in

WEIGHT 145 lbs

BASE New York City

ALLIES Justice Society of America

FOES Vandal Savage

Tomcat's ferocious teeth and claws frighten his enemies into submission.

POWERS: In his were-cat form, Tomcat has super-strength, agility, and enhanced senses. He also has sharp teeth and claws, as well as a tail that can catch hold of things and whip his opponents. Though not keen on fighting at first, Tomcat has learned hand-to-hand combat techniques from his father.

LIKE FATHER, LIKE SON?
Prior to joining the Justice Society, Tomcat's life lacked serious direction. When it was revealed that Wildcat was his father, Tomcat saw this as an opportunity to find out who he really was and discover what he could achieve as a hero.

THE TRICKSTER
PRANKSTER PEST

Axel Walker is a mischievous teenager who stole many dangerous gadgets from James Jesse, the original Trickster. After deciding that the reformed Jesse no longer deserved the title, Axel became the all-new Trickster and began a crime-filled career, joining the Flash's Rogues Gallery of villains.

VITAL STATS
REAL NAME Axel Walker
OCCUPATION Villain
HEIGHT 5ft 7in
WEIGHT 150 lbs
BASE Keystone City
ALLIES The Rogues
FOES The Flash, Kid Flash

The Trickster keeps his pranking equipment with him when committing a crime.

His anti-gravity boots allow him to walk on air.

JAMES JESSE
For many years, James Jesse fought the Flash as the first villainous Trickster. After becoming convinced that crime doesn't pay, Jesse used his inside knowledge of the criminal underworld to become an FBI investigator. Now he even assists the Flash on some cases!

POWERS: While the Trickster possesses no superpowers, he's still considered extremely dangerous. He uses a variety of sinister gadgets such as exploding gum, itching power, and spiked jacks to perform his pranks. The Trickster's impulsive behavior has often put him—and innocent bystanders—in the line of fire.

TRIGON
DEMON LORD

Trigon is a cruel and powerful conqueror who was born when the evil energies of another dimension came together in demon form. He seeks to cast darkness over the Earth, having already conquered many other worlds. Trigon has often tried to manipulate his daughter, Raven, in his quest for ultimate power.

Trigon can project destructive energy beams from his four eyes.

He has the ablity to shift his size, quickly becoming a giant.

VITAL STATS
REAL NAME Trigon
OCCUPATION Demon
HEIGHT Variable
WEIGHT Variable
BASE Azarath
ALLIES Brother Blood
FOES Raven, Teen Titans

POWERS: Trigon is an all-powerful being who possesses super-strength and is practically invulnerable. He's a skilled illusion-caster and often disguises himself to gain the trust of humans. Trigon can also pass his po~~ ~~ his offspring, though ~~ ~~ this po~~

SONS OF TRIGON
Once, when Trigon sought to invade Earth, he enlisted his three sons to help retrieve the power that he needed. Instead, they betrayed him and took the power for themselves— an act that secretly made the evil

TWO-FACE
DOUBLE-SIDED TROUBLE

Harvey Dent was a respected attorney who fought hard to bring criminals to justice—until a vengeful mob boss threw acid in his face. Harvey was scarred both physically and mentally. He turned into a mad criminal called Two-Face who makes life and death decisions based only on the flip of a coin.

VITAL STATS

REAL NAME Harvey Dent
OCCUPATION Villain
HEIGHT 6ft
WEIGHT 182 lbs
BASE Gotham City
ALLIES Hush
FOES Batman, Nightwing

He wears a specially tailored suit that reflects his split personality.

Two-Face doesn't feel complete without his two-headed coin.

DEADLY ORIGINS

Crime lord Sal Maroni believed lawyer Harvey Dent was responsible for his father's death. So, in an act of vengeance, Maroni threw acid in Dent's face. This villainous act ruined Dent's features and fractured his mind, causing him to become the unstable Two-Face.

POWERS: Two-Face suffers from a multiple personality disorder which causes his mind to split into different personas. As Harvey Dent he's cool, calm, and collected—but as Two-Face he's dangerous and destructive. Two-Face is so obsessed with duality that he flips a coin to decide whether he will be good or evil.

ULTRA-HUMANITE

GIFTED GORILLA

Ultra-Humanite has the power to tranfer his brain into any physical body.

Scientist Gerard Shugel's body was stricken with a terrible disease, so he transferred his super-intelligent brain into the body of a rare white gorilla. Now as the super-strong Ultra-Humanite, he travels through time hoping to find the perfect era in which he can conquer the Earth.

His gorilla body is very agile—a sure advantage in battle.

VITAL STATS

REAL NAME Gerard Shugel
OCCUPATION Scientist, Villain
HEIGHT 6ft 4in
WEIGHT 476 lbs
BASE Mobile
ALLIES Time Stealers, Injustice Society
FOES Power Girl, Justice Society of America

BODY SNATCHER
Ultra-Humanite has transferred his brain into many bodies over the years in an effort to evade capture. He has been a giant insect and a Tyrannosaurus Rex. He once masqueraded as beautiful actress Dolores Winters and even inhabited the body of the hero Johnny Thunder for a short time.

POWERS: Ultra-Humanite might look like a gorilla, but he has the genius-level intellect of his original form—a gifted scientist and inventor. He also possesses low-level telepathic skills. Ultra-Humanite's mutated gorilla body is incredibly strong and durable, making him an above-average hand-to-hand combatant.

VANDAL SAVAGE
ETERNAL CONQUEROR

In prehistoric times, Vandal Savage was a mere caveman. When a meteorite struck the Earth, it showered Vandal with radiation that gave him the ability to live forever. Over the centuries, Vandal has gone by many names and conquered many lands, but the Justice Society heroes are always there to try and stop him.

VITAL STATS
REAL NAME Vandar Adg
OCCUPATION Conqueror
HEIGHT 5ft 10in
WEIGHT 170 lbs
BASE Mobile
ALLIES Secret Society of Super-Villains, Tartarus
FOES Justice Society of America, Resurrection Man

One of Vandal's most powerful weapons is his brilliant tactical mind.

Vandal's body is thousands of years old, although his organs have been replaced.

CAVEMAN
Over 50,000 years ago, at the dawn of humanity, Vandal Savage led the band of cavemen known as the Blood Tribe. Though he seems to have evolved through the years, Savage still retains a primal, vicious streak—and an unquenchable thirst for battle.

POWERS: Vandal Savage is a brilliant strategist who has orchestrated and won a multitude of wars during his time on Earth. He's also a scientist with knowledge of the mystical arts. Though Vandal is immortal, he must continually replace his internal organs of his descendants to stay alive.

VENTRILOQUIST AND SCARFACE
VOICE OF CRIME

Peyton Riley was married to a mobster from a top Gotham City crime family. When her husband tried to have her destroyed, she was saved by Scarface, an evil puppet in need of a new master. Under his influence, Peyton became the Ventriloquist, his intelligent and glamorous partner-in-crime.

Scarface is made from cursed wood.

The Ventriloquist's blonde hair hides a terrible scar.

Scarface carries a Tommy Gun for protection.

VITAL STATS

VENTRILOQUIST
REAL NAME Peyton Riley
OCCUPATION Villain
HEIGHT 5ft 8in
WEIGHT 140 lbs
BASE Gotham City
ALLIES Quakemaster
FOES Batman

SCARFACE
HEIGHT 3ft
WEIGHT 6 lbs

ARNOLD WESKER
Scarface's previous partner was drug lord Arnold Wesker, the first Ventriloquist. Together they ran a massive criminal empire—until the Great White Shark had Wesker removed in an attempt to seize control of Gotham City's underworld.

POWERS: The Ventriloquist suffers from a condition that gives her an alternate personality that she voices through her puppet, Scarface. When manipulating the puppet, she throws her voice so expertly that it seems as though Scarface is speaking. The Ventriloquist is also a cunning criminal genius.

VIXEN
BEAUTY AND THE BEASTS

Supermodel Mari McCabe inherited a magical totem, passed down through her family by the spider-god Anansi. Using the totem she became Vixen, a hero who can harness the powers of the animal kingdom. Vixen joined the Justice League of America where she uses her abilities to protect the innocent.

VITAL STATS

REAL NAME Mari Jiwe McCabe

OCCUPATION Hero

HEIGHT 5ft 7in

WEIGHT 149 lbs

BASE Mobile

ALLIES Animal Man, Justice Society of America

FOES Anansi

The Tantu totem is shaped like a fox's head.

Her claws can tear through metal.

Vixen must be within 150 feet of an animal to mimic its abilities.

STOLEN TOTEM
When Professor Ivo attempted to destroy the Justice League, he stole Vixen's Tantu Totem and implanted it inside Amazo. Vixen's powers became erratic, but through an investigation she was able to find Amazo and destroy him, retrieving her totem in the process.

POWERS: Vixen is able to mimic the abilities of any animal she chooses using the power of her mystical Tantu Totem—though she can only channel the power of one animal at a time. Whether she has the strength of a rhino, the speed of cheetah, or the flying prowess of a hawk, Vixen is a force to be reckoned with.

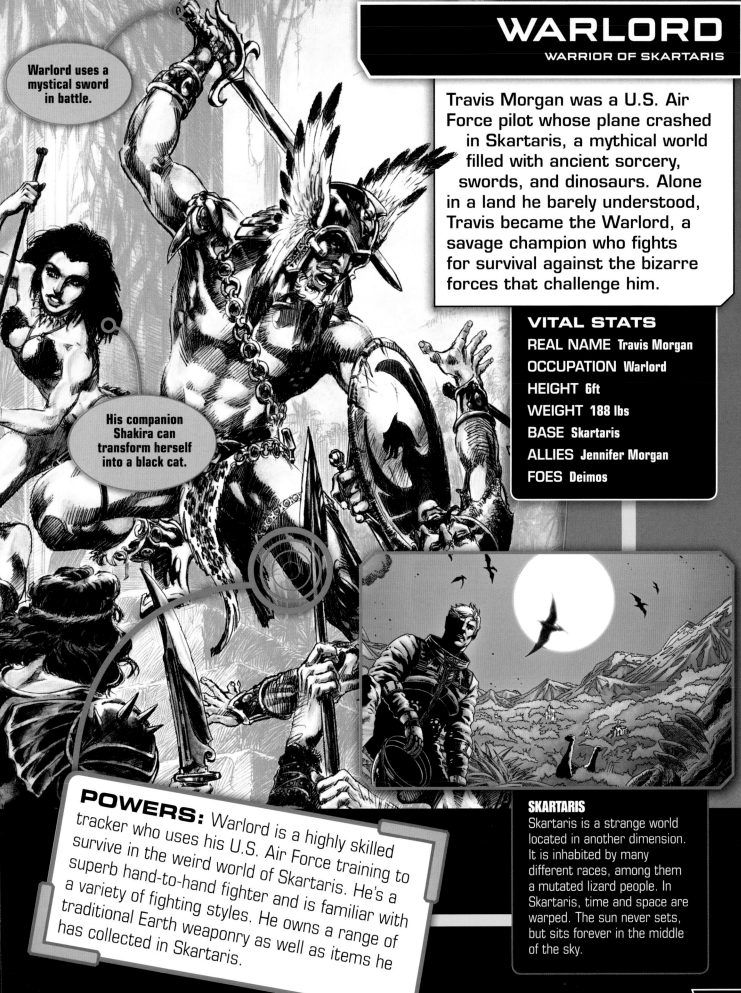

Warlord uses a mystical sword in battle.

WARLORD
WARRIOR OF SKARTARIS

Travis Morgan was a U.S. Air Force pilot whose plane crashed in Skartaris, a mythical world filled with ancient sorcery, swords, and dinosaurs. Alone in a land he barely understood, Travis became the Warlord, a savage champion who fights for survival against the bizarre forces that challenge him.

His companion Shakira can transform herself into a black cat.

VITAL STATS
REAL NAME Travis Morgan
OCCUPATION Warlord
HEIGHT 6ft
WEIGHT 188 lbs
BASE Skartaris
ALLIES Jennifer Morgan
FOES Deimos

POWERS: Warlord is a highly skilled tracker who uses his U.S. Air Force training to survive in the weird world of Skartaris. He's a superb hand-to-hand fighter and is familiar with a variety of fighting styles. He owns a range of traditional Earth weaponry as well as items he has collected in Skartaris.

SKARTARIS
Skartaris is a strange world located in another dimension. It is inhabited by many different races, among them a mutated lizard people. In Skartaris, time and space are warped. The sun never sets, but sits forever in the middle of the sky.

WEATHER WIZARD
CLIMATE-CONTROLLING CRIMINAL

Criminal Mark Mardon escaped prison and planned to hide out at his scientist brother's house. There he found secret plans for a weather-controlling device. Mardon used the plans to build a wand that enabled him to manipulate the elements. Now known as the Weather Wizard, he is a frequent foe of the Flash.

VITAL STATS

REAL NAME Mark Mardon
OCCUPATION Villain
HEIGHT 6ft 1in
WEIGHT 185 lbs
BASE Central City
ALLIES The Rogues
FOES The Flash, Kid Flash

Weather Wizard has now learned to control the weather without using a wand.

WIND WARFARE
When the Weather Wizard learned that his son possessed natural weather-controlling powers, he abducted the boy. The Flash was able to protect the child from harm, but the Weather Wizard swore vengeance. He has since joined the villainous Rogues group to see his vow realized.

POWERS: Weather Wizard used a special wand that can control the elements. He's able to summon tornadoes and cause rainstorms and blizzards. He can also harness electrical energy to generate lightning bolts. Thanks to futuristic magic, Weather Wizard doesn't need his wand any longer.

WILDCAT
LEGEND IN THE RING

Ted Grant was a prize-winning boxer who was framed for a crime he didn't commit. So Ted donned a costume, adopted the persona of Wildcat, and joined the Justice Society of America where he was able to clear his name. Wildcat uses his expert combat knowledge to train the next generation of heroes.

VITAL STATS

REAL NAME Ted Grant
OCCUPATION Boxer, Hero
HEIGHT 6ft 5in
WEIGHT 250 lbs
BASE New York City
ALLIES Justice Society of America
FOES Golden Wasp

POWERS: Wildcat is highly skilled in almost all forms of hand-to-hand combat, though he prefers simple street-fighting in battle. He also has above-average strength and durability, having seen his fair share of action in the boxing ring. Wildcat recently discovered that he has mysteriously acquired nine lives.

HERO TRAINER
Over the years, Wildcat has trained heroes like Batman and Huntress, and he enjoys giving them tips on how to beat their opponents. Wildcat's fighting style is unmatched. Even his superpowered teammates in the JSA find it difficult to go toe-to-toe with him in the boxing ring!

WONDER GIRL
DAUGHTER OF ZEUS

Young Cassie Sandsmark was given powers by her father Zeus, the king of the gods. She became the hero known as Wonder Girl. Though her human mother sometimes worries about the dangers she faces in battle, Wonder Girl always feels supported by her fellow heroes, the Teen Titans.

VITAL STATS

REAL NAME Cassandra "Cassie" Sandsmark

OCCUPATION Hero

HEIGHT 5ft 4in

WEIGHT 130 lbs

BASE San Francisco

ALLIES Wonder Woman, Teen Titans

FOES Ares, Silver Swan

Wonder Girl's electrified lasso was a gift from her half-brother, Ares.

YOUNGER YEARS
During her early days as Wonder Girl, Cassandra wore a black wig to conceal her identity. She also wore the Sandals of Hermes—a gift from Zeus—to help her fly. Eventually she grew into her role and shed her bulky costume.

POWERS: Wonder Girl possesses super-strength and super-speed as well as the power of flight, though her abilities continue to develop. She has had extensive combat training and knows a number of martial arts disciplines. Wonder Girl also uses a lasso that can produce a powerful lightning strike, shocking her enemies.

WONDER WOMAN
AMAZON PRINCESS

Wonder Woman was sculpted from the magical clay of the island Themyscira and given life by the Gods of Olympus. She's an ambassador of peace and justice in the modern world, but often has to put her warrior training to good use. Wonder Woman is a founding member of the Justice League of America.

VITAL STATS
REAL NAME Diana Prince
OCCUPATION Ambassador of Peace
HEIGHT 6ft
WEIGHT 165 lbs
BASE Themyscira
ALLIES Wonder Girl, Donna Troy
FOES Circe, Ares, Cheetah

No one can lie when bound by her golden Lasso of Truth.

Wonder Woman's wrist gauntlets deflect bullets.

CHAMPION OF FREEDOM
Diana became Wonder Woman after her mother held a contest of skill to choose an Amazonian ambassador to send to the outside world. Though Diana was forbidden to participate, she disguised herself and ultimately won the contest—much to her mother's frustration.

POWERS: Wonder Woman has super-strength, super-speed, and a healing factor which protects her from harm. As an Amazon warrior, she has trained in multiple forms of hand-to-hand combat. Wonder Woman also possesses the power to communicate with nature and to empathize with animals.

ZATANNA
MISTRESS OF MAGIC

Zatanna is a world-famous sorceress and magician who followed in the footsteps of Giovanni Zatara, her warlock father, and became a hero. Though Zatanna enjoys putting on elaborate magic shows, she also fights the forces of evil as a member of the Justice League.

VITAL STATS

REAL NAME Zatanna Zatara
OCCUPATION Magician, Hero
HEIGHT 5ft 7in
WEIGHT 135 lbs
BASE San Francisco
ALLIES Batman, Justice League of America
FOES Hush, Brother Night

When casting spells, Zatanna recites them in backwards English.

Zatanna's costume reflects her identity as a theatrical stage magician.

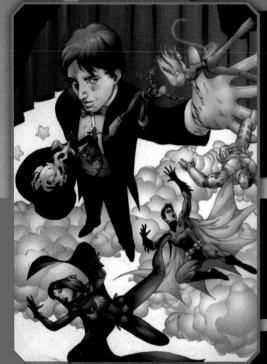

ZACHARY ZATARA
Zatanna has some competition from her cousin and fellow magician, Zachary Zatara. The aloof Zachary sees himself as the superior spell-caster of the Zatara family. But thankfully, Zatanna and Zachary's Teen Titans friends are there to put him in his place.

POWERS: Zatanna is an excellent spell-caster, and prefers to work her magic by reciting spells backwards. She is highly trained in sleight-of-hand magic, specializing in large-scale illusions. Zatanna can read minds and alter a person's thoughts and actions, though she is ...tant to use these particular powers.

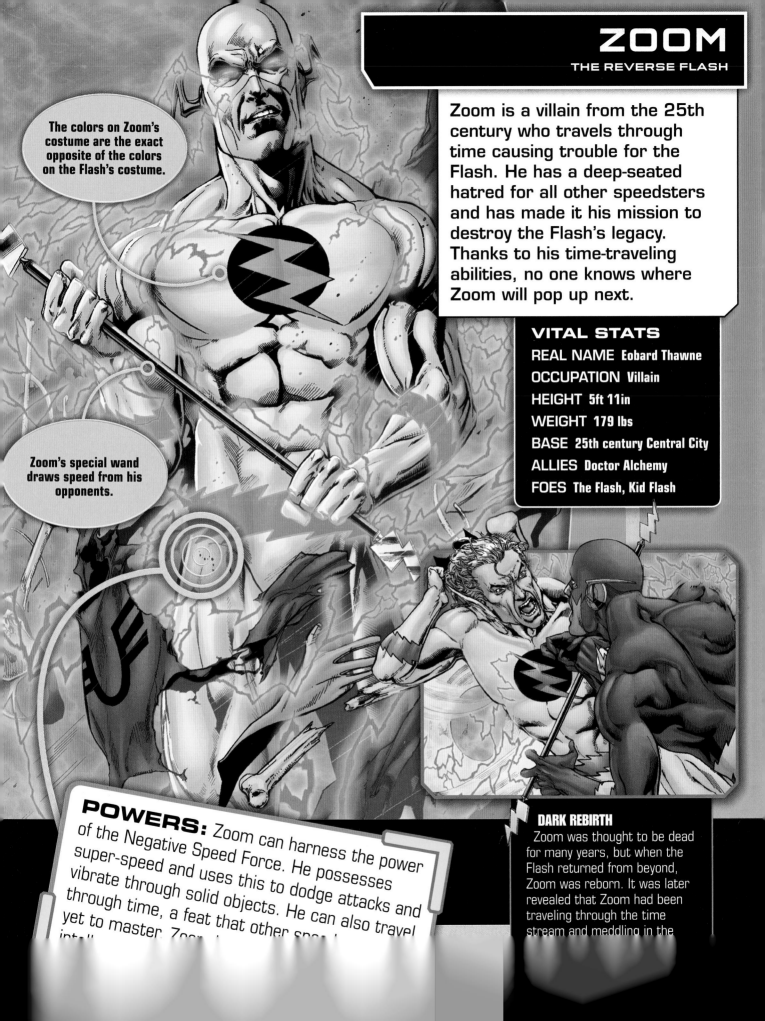

ZOOM
THE REVERSE FLASH

Zoom is a villain from the 25th century who travels through time causing trouble for the Flash. He has a deep-seated hatred for all other speedsters and has made it his mission to destroy the Flash's legacy. Thanks to his time-traveling abilities, no one knows where Zoom will pop up next.

The colors on Zoom's costume are the exact opposite of the colors on the Flash's costume.

Zoom's special wand draws speed from his opponents.

VITAL STATS
REAL NAME Eobard Thawne
OCCUPATION Villain
HEIGHT 5ft 11in
WEIGHT 179 lbs
BASE 25th century Central City
ALLIES Doctor Alchemy
FOES The Flash, Kid Flash

POWERS: Zoom can harness the power of the Negative Speed Force. He possesses super-speed and uses this to dodge attacks and vibrate through solid objects. He can also travel through time, a feat that other spee... yet to master. Zoom i...
int...

DARK REBIRTH
Zoom was thought to be dead for many years, but when the Flash returned from beyond, Zoom was reborn. It was later revealed that Zoom had been traveling through the time stream and meddling in the

LONDON, NEW YORK,
MELBOURNE, MUNICH, AND DELHI

EDITORS: Shari Last, Julia March
SENIOR DESIGNER: Robert Perry
DESIGN ASSISTANT: Rhys Thomas
MANAGING ART EDITOR: Ron Stobbart
PUBLISHING MANAGER: Catherine Saunders
ART DIRECTOR: Lisa Lanzarini
PUBLISHER: Simon Beecroft
PUBLISHING DIRECTOR: Alex Allan
PRODUCTION EDITOR: Siu Yin Chan
PRODUCTION CONTROLLER: Nick Seston

This edition published in 2013
First published in Great Britain in 2011 by
Dorling Kindersley Limited
80 Strand, London WC2R ORL
Penguin Group (UK)

10 9 8 7 6 5 4 3 2 1
001-179625-Sep/13

A CIP catalogue record for this book
is available from the British Library.

ISBN: 978-1-4093-4246-5

Colour reproduction by Media Development Printing, UK
Printed and bound by Hung Hing, China

Dorling Kindersley would like to thank:
Frank Pittarese – Editor, DC Comics;
Victoria Taylor and Meredith Greenberg for editorial assistance.

Discover more at
www.dk.com

ARTIST ACKNOWLEDGEMENTS

Daniel Acuña, Arthur Adams, Christian Alamy, Oclair Albert, Rafael Albuquerque, Quique Alcatena, Bob Almond, Marlo Alquiza, Murphy Anderson, Jim Aparo, Renato Arlem, Mahmud Asrar, Derec Aucoin, Terry Austin, Mark Bagley, Michael Bair, Matt Banning, Eddy Barrows, Chris Batista, Ed Benes, Mariah Benes, Joe Benitez, Josep Beroy, Patrick Blaine, Fernando Blanco, Brian Bolland, Geraldo Borjes, Brett Breeding, Rebecca Buchman, Mark Buckingham, John Byrne, Jim Calafiore, Matt Camp, Robert Campanella, Marc Campos, Mauro Cascioli, John Cassaday, Claudio Castellini, Anthony Castrillo, Keith Champagne, Bernard Chang, Sean Chen, Cliff Chiang, Frank Chiaramonte, Ian Churchill, Vicente Cifuentes, Yildiray Cinar, Matthew Clark, Andy Clarke, Amanda Conner, Richard Corben, CrisCross, Steven Cummings, Fernando Dagnino, Tony S. Daniel, Alan Davis, Dan Davis, Shane Davis, Mike DeCarlo, John Dell, Jesse Delperdang, Mike Deodato Jr., Tom Derenick, Rachel Dodson, Terry Dodson, Dale Eaglesham, Mark Farmer, Wayne Faucher, Duncan Fegredo, Lee Ferguson, Raul Fernandez, Julio Ferreira, Pascal Ferry, David Finch, Fabrizio Fiorentino, Max Fiumara, Sandu Florea, Gary Frank, Richard Friend, Lee Garbett, Manuel Garcia, José Luis García-López, Alex Garner, Keith Giffen, Dick Giordano, Jonathan Glapion, Patrick Gleason, Dan Green, Sanford Greene, Mike Grell, Tom Grindberg, Renato Guedes, Yvel Guichet, Paul Gulacy, Cully Hamner, Scott Hanna, Chad Hardin, Jeremy Haun, Doug Hazlewood, Adam Hughes, Rob Hunter, Jamal Igle, Jack Jadson, Dennis Janke, Klaus Janson, Phil Jimenez, J.G. Jones, Ruy Jose, Dan Jurgens, Justiniano, Gil Kane, Kano, Karl Kesel, Jack Kirby, Leonard Kirk, Scott Koblish, Scott Kolins, Don Kramer, Adam Kubert, Andy Kubert, Greg Land, Andy Lanning, Michael Lark, Ken Lashley, Stanley Lau, Jim Lee, Jay Leisten, Rob Liefeld, Steve Lightle, John Livesay, Julian Lopez, Aaron Lopresti, John Lucas, Daniel LuVisi, Jose Wilson Magalhaés, Carlos Magno, Kevin Maguire, Larry Mahlstedt, Pop Mahn, Doug Mahnke, Francis Manapul, Tom Mandrake, Guillem March, Nathan Massengill, Francesco Mattina, Ray McCarthy, Scott McDaniel, Ed McGuiness, Mark McKenna, Mike McKone, Shawn McManus, Jesus Merino, Joshua Middleton, Lee Moder, Sheldon Moldoff, Mark Morales, Rags Morales, Diogenes Neves, Tom Nguyen, Phil Noto, Kevin Nowlan, Ariel Olivetti, Jerry Ordway, Andy Owens, Carlos Pacheco, Jimmy Palmiotti, Dan Panosian, Eduardo Pansica, Fernando Pasarin, Paul Pelletier, George Pérez, Brandon Peterson, Joe Phillips, Javier Pina, Howard Porter, Eric Powell, Joe Prado, Mark Propst, Howard Purcell, Jack Purcell, Joe Quesada, Frank Quitely, Stefano Raffaele, Pablo Raimondi, Rodney Ramos, Tom Raney, Norm Rapmund, Amy Reeder, Ivan Reis, Cliff Richards, Robin Riggs, Darick Robertson, Kenneth Rocafort, Carlos Rodriguez, Hannibal Rodriguez, Jason Rodriguez, Prentis Rollins, Alex Ross, Duncan Rouleau, Stephane Roux, Mike Royer, Matt Ryan, Bernard Sachs, Stephen Sadowski, Jesus Saiz, Chris Samnee, Amilton Santos, Nicola Scott, Trevor Scott, Stephen Jorge Segovia, Mike Sekowsky, Kevin Sharpe, Jon Sibal, Walter Simonson, Paulo Siqueira, Cam Smith, John K. Snyder III, Jim Starlin, Brian Stelfreeze, John Stokes, Karl Story, Rob Stull, Ardian Syaf, Philip Tan, Romeo Tanghal, Mark Texeira, Art Thibert, Jill Thompson, Bruce W. Timm, Marcus To, Billy Tucci, Michael Turner, Angel Unzueta, Ethan Van Sciver, Sal Velluto, Dexter Vines, Brad Walker, Lee Weeks, Freddie Williams II, J.H. Williams III, Scott Williams, Phil Winslade, Stan Woch, Walden Wong, Pete Woods, Chris Wozniak.